Digital Culture & Society

Vol 8, Issue 2/2022

Mathias Fuchs, Karin Wenz (eds.)
Algorithmic Art

The journal is edited by
Mathias Fuchs, Ramón Reichert, and Karin Wenz

Editorial Board
Maria Bakardjeva, David Berry, Jean Burgess, Mark Coté, Colin Cremin, Sean Cubitt, Mark Deuze, José van Dijck, Delia Dumitrica, Astrid Ensslin, Sonia Fizek, Federica Frabetti, Orit Halpern, Irina Kaldrack, Denisa Kera, Lev Manovich, Janet H. Murray, Jussi Parikka, Lisa Parks, Dominic Pettman, Rita Raley, Richard Rogers, Julian Rohrhuber, Marie-Laure Ryan, Mirko Tobias Schäfer, Jens Schröter, Trebor Scholz, Tamar Sharon, Roberto Simanowski, Nathaniel Takcz, Geoffrey Winthrop-Young, Sally Wyatt

[transcript]

Indexed in EBSCOhost databases

Bibliographic information published by the Deutsche Nationalbibliothek
The Deutsche Nationalbibliothek lists this publication in the Deutsche National-
bibliografie; detailed bibliographic data are available on the Internet at http://
dnb.d-nb.de

© 2023 transcript Verlag, Bielefeld

All rights reserved. No part of this book may be reprinted or reproduced or utilized in any form or by any electronic, mechanical, or other means, now known or hereafter invented, including photocopying and recording, or in any information storage or retrieval system, without permission in writing from the publisher.

Cover concept: Kordula Röckenhaus, Bielefeld
Typeset: Mark-Sebastian Schneider, Bielefeld

ISSN: 2364-2114
eISSN: 2364-2122
Print-ISBN 978-3-8376-5904-7
PDF-ISBN 978-3-8394-5904-1

Content

Introduction
Algorithmic Art. Past and Contemporary Perspectives
Mathias Fuchs and Karin Wenz   5

I Artists' Statements

Artificial Intelligence as Phármakon
Algorithmic Art between Remedy and Poison
Giselle Beiguelman   15

Impressionistic Programming
Aesthetical and technical methods for creating the interactive artwork "Portrait on the Fly"
Laurent Mignonneau and Christa Sommerer   25

Against the Norm
Othering and Otherness in AI Aesthetics
Marco Donnarumma   39

The Dancer in the Machine
Simon Biggs, Sue Hawksley and Mark D. McDonnell   67

II History and Theory of Algorithmic Art

Web Search Fever and Collecting as the Human Condition
Patricia de Vries   87

Cybernetics and the early experiments in Computer Art
Angela Krewani   107

A Slightly Off Performance
Some Observations on Algorithmic Translation as/in Artistic Practice
Anna Luhn   123

III Literature Survey

Literature Survey
1950s to the Present
Mathias Fuchs   143

Biographical Notes   153

Introduction
Algorithmic Art. Past and Contemporary Perspectives

Mathias Fuchs and Karin Wenz

In his 1993 book *Art of the Electronic Age* Frank Popper tells us that "[t]he origins of Computer Art can be traced back to 1952 when Ben F. Laposky, in the U.S.A., used an analogic computer and a cathode tube oscillograph for the composition of his *Electronic Abstractions*." (1993: 78) Already in the 30s of the last century Bense and Birkhoff developed an aesthetic theory based on arithmetic operations long before the Personal Computer and networked connectivity were at the horizon of imagination. In the context of computer art, Max Bense explored the potential of computers as tools for artistic creation and expression (cf. Bense 1956; 1998). Bense's works laid the groundwork for his ideas on computer-generated art and the role of algorithms in artistic creation. His reflections on computer art focused on the theoretical and philosophical implications rather than practical implementation. He believed that computers could assist artists in generating complex and precise aesthetic forms, but he also emphasized the need for human creativity and judgment in the artistic process.

Bense's interest in computer art stemmed from his broader philosophical framework, which emphasized the relationship between information theory, cybernetics, and aesthetics. He argued that art should be based on scientific principles and that aesthetic judgments could be objectively made based on mathematical criteria. (Krewani 2016: 111-12)

Max Bense's ideas and contributions had a significant impact, especially on the development of computer art in Germany and in Brazil. His work influenced a generation of German and Brazilian artists, scholars, and theorists who were interested in exploring the intersection of technology, aesthetics, and artistic expression.

His concepts helped shape the discourse surrounding computer art especially in Brazil and inspired artists to explore new possibilities offered by computers and algorithms. Bense's influence on Brazilian computer art extended beyond the artistic realm. His concepts were also embraced by scholars and researchers working in the fields of semiotics, aesthetics, media theory, and digital culture. His interdisciplinary approach, combining philosophy, information theory, and art, resonated with the intellectual climate in Brazil, contributing to the development of a rich and diverse discourse around computer art. (Cordeiro 1972, see also Kac 2007 and Beiguelmann in this special issue). While Bense contributed to the theoretical framework of computer art, he was not a practicing artist in the traditional sense. His focus was primarily on the philosophical and theoretical aspects of aesthetics and the potential of computers in art.

The 1960s were also the time when practicing artists started to create works of algorithmic art with graphic work by Vera Molnár, Frieder Nake, Georg Nees, Michael Noll, K.C. Knowlton, Herbert W. Franke, and others. What started as experimental work with digital computers and output devices of that time, soon spread into the realms of music, poetry, sculpture, and architecture. Popper sees five different areas, the computer can intervene in: "plastic, film, or video images; in cybernetic sculptures; in environmental artworks; in optical or video discs; and in telecommunication events." (ibid.) Even seen from the viewpoint of the 1990s, Popper obviously forgot to mention sound and text compositions generated with the aid of algorithms. Today artists use programmes for the generation of text, image and sound, sculptures, architecture, installations, web-based pieces, performance, game art, and bioart. Obviously, the range of mediatic approaches towards algorithmic art is wider now than it was then. Yet, some of the questions regarding authorship, aesthetic value, socio-political relevance and interdependencies of art and technology remain essential. This issue of the *Journal Digital Culture and Society* does not intend to celebrate the latest software achievements in the field of AI, image generation or pop-musical pastiche, but it rather opens a discussion about the aesthetic and socio-political implications of algorithmic art, it showcases work of artists who use computing machinery for their pieces, and it presents theoretical considerations with the history of algorithmic art in mind.

Algorithmic art, computer art, computer-aided artistic practice, digital art, cybernetic art, or electronic art? Please, read the chapter *Literature Survey* at the end of this journal to get an attempt of explanation, why and when the terminological turn switched focus from computer art towards algorithmic art. The editors decided to give this issue of the *Journal Digital Culture and Society* the title "Algorithmic Art" – reassured by Hans Ulrich Reck's warning in the *Myth of Media Art* (2007) that we should better not talk about "oil art" when we speak about landscape painting. By analogy "computer art" would be too close a term to the machine, when the algorithmic formalisation is of interest. Compare the example of Kurt Ingerl's pre-PC algorithmic sculptures (Fig.1, below).

What did change in the practice and public appreciation of art produced with the assistance of digital computers during the last 60 years? There can be no doubt that computational complexity has increased dramatically. It is also pertinent to note that complete control of a few lines of code by the "algorists" of the 1960s (Jean-Pierre Hébert 1995; Frieder Nake 2012), i.e. the artists producing output with the assistance of computers.

Jean-Pierre Hébert's manifesto-definition of an algorist reads:

```
if (creation && object of art && algorithm && one's own algorithm)
{ include * an algorist * }
```

elseif (!creation || !object of art || !algorithm || !one's own algorithm)
{ exclude * not an algorist * }

Hébert identifies artists who create an object of art with a process that includes their own algorithms as algorists.

The algorist has nowadays been replaced by calls of software systems that are no longer one man's or woman's crafted products. Artists working in algorithmic art often embrace concepts such as emergence, self-organization, and generativity, allowing the artwork to evolve or adapt based on predetermined rules or interactions with the audience or the environment. The artists whose production relies on software systems, some of them algorithmic power-tools, can use these tools in a creative, subversive, or critical manner, but they are by no means directors of the output in a bit-to-bit or pixel-by-pixel control.

The term algorithm goes back to Muhammad ibn Musa al-Khwarizmi's *kitāb al-ḥisāb al-hindī* (*Book of Indian computation*) and *Summation and Subtraction in Indian Arithmetic* from around 825. What made al-Khwarizmi's writings so important was the fact that he could show that computation was not based on intelligence, intuition, or genius, but rather on an automatable procedure that would render results without any human interference. This is what the pioneers of information theory picked up upon. (Bense 1956; 1998, Birkhoff 1929; 1931; 1933) Could it be possible to compute aesthetics as a matter of information content, redundancy, probabilities? Abraham A. Moles thought so: "The definition of beauty is a consequence of the statistics of beautiful objects." (1973: 95) Moles states that this new way of understanding aesthetics has not been considered by theoreticians. "[T]he idea of numeric assessment does not match easily with the transcendental. Philosophers have cherished the latter, but beauty is closely related to society. Beauty is at the crossroads of many individual thoughts." (ibid.) Moles comprehends algorithmic art as emancipatory. He praises random permutations in the production of art as a "marvellous game" (ibid.: 94). Enthusiastically he spins his thoughts about "creative machines" (ibid.: 95) that will be able to provide every department store customer with a formica plate for his kitchen table "with a unique and distinctive pattern of personally designed inlay work, produced exclusively for him by the artist-machine." (ibid.: 94) For Moles, Bense and Nake it was obvious that algorithmic art could lead to a democratisation of society. What Moles labelled "Neo-Cartesianism", was close to the "existential rationalism" Bense promoted. Frieder Nake, finally choose the political view of Maoism and joined the Communist Association of West Germany (LBW: Kommunistischer Bund Westdeutschland). For him algorithmic art was part of the "algorithmic revolution" (Nake 2016).

The permutational pieces of the 1960s and 1970s have not been produced to celebrate an individual artist's masterpiece.[1] The have rather been set up as multiples. "Art is the creation of models that are destined to be reproduced." (Moles 1973: 99) Walter Benjamin's *The Work of Art in the Age of Mechanical Reproduction* (1935) obviously influenced Abraham André Moles, and Max Bense explicitely referred to Benjamin's concept of art and technology. Artists' algorithms were thought to produce "art for the masses in a mass society" (Moles 1973: 99) and Franke's woven textiles, Moles' formica plates for department store customers, or Kurt Ingerl's sculptural experiments were examples for un-pretentious, pragmatic everyday design made with the generative support of algorithms. Kurt Ingerl's façade for a building in Vienna's 14th district was based on algorithms the sculptor wrote himself with the aid of pen and paper – before he finally had access to a computer in the year 1974.

Fig. 1: An algorithmically generated facade by Kurt Ingerl in Vienna's Hackengasse. Photo © Mathias Fuchs 2021.

NFTs (Non-Fungible Tokens) have had a significant impact on the world of computer art in recent years. NFTs are digital assets that represent ownership or proof of authenticity for unique items or works, typically using blockchain tech-

---

1   It is only in this decade that some of the works by Vera Molnár, Herbert W. Franke a.o. are shown at art fairs with a price tag on them (e.g. at viennacontemporary 2021).

nology. They have gained attention for their role in the art market, particularly for algorithmic artworks. Computer art has found a natural fit with NFTs. The possible implementation of blockchain technology in the art world, is according to some scholars "one of the least discussed applications for blockchain, yet one where the technology may hit hardest." (MacDonald-Korth/Lehdonvirta/Meyer 2018: 5) Although far from mainstream reach, applications of blockchain technologies in the arts have gained traction in recent years. The shared belief and anticipation of the disruptive potential of blockchain technologies, outside of strictly commercial logics and financial services, has come with the emergence of the art-tech start-up, and with numerous dedicated conferences and public events by high-profile art institutions that anticipate the possible fruitful avenues of the encounter and intertwinement of the art world and blockchain technology.

The tension lies between the reproducibility of algorithmic art versus the "scarcity-equals-value paradigm" which governs much of the art market. As Zanni (2018) explains, art galleries and collectors are still obsessed with the idea of a unique, singular, one of its kind art objects and its perceived auratic characteristics, which makes for a unique selling point, an overseeable art market, and enhances "the status of the owner" (p.19). This explains the recent hype about NFTs and the discussions about contemporary computer art demonstrate that algorithmic works of art have regained their relevance for the art markets. Computer art, it seems, has lost the innocence of pure aesthetic speculation, it reunited with ideas of the genius, the owner, the masterpiece, individuality, and the price. The editors of this issue of the *Journal Digital Culture and Society* did on purpose not showcase the NFTs, that sell for millions of dollars, collectibles hyped by fan communities, but selected excellent artists who produce conceptionally well-considered pieces. The work displayed here and introduced by the artists challenges our understanding of what algorithms can do, when used in an innovative and well-informed manner.

The first article in this journal's issue is the presentation of Giselle Beiguelman's recent investigation into text-to-image and image-to-text tools. The images that you will find here are obviously statements that refer to colonial history, to rituals, plant power, prohibition, and interdictions. A short text by the artist provides clues to the background Beiguelman is working from.

Also concerned about cultural biases and post-colonial power structures is Marco Donnarumma, an artist himself, who reflects about *the Other* and *Otherness* in his text. Marco Donnarumma decided to not present his own work, but he provided us with a link to an online documentation featuring some of his work. (Point your browser to https://marcodonnarumma.com/) Donnarumma investigates the connection between science, episteme, and aesthetics as shown by large deep learning models with a focus on AI image generators. He claims that these AI image generators and the results they produce need to be investigated as expressions of normative power.

Christa Sommerer and Laurent Mignonneau have been working in the field of algorithmic art and in particular in generative art and flora and fauna simulations, first in Japan then in other places and now in Linz/ Austria. We first met Christa and Laurent in ATR Media Integration and Communications Research Lab next to Kyoto, Japan, many years ago and are glad to see that they won – or rather achieved without any reservations – the Austrian State Art Price for their long years of developing outstanding work. (Österreichischer Staatskunstpreis for Christa Sommerer und Laurent Mignonneau)

The article by Simon Biggs, Sue Hawskley and Marc D. McDonnell discusses creativity, agency, and AI, specifically concept of distributed agency in human and non-humans is examined. The focus is on the interactive artwork called *Double Agent*, created by Simon Biggs. This artwork is not only used as a case study for exploring the topic but also as an example for a theoretical discussion of creativity, agency, and ontology, drawing on N. Katherine Hayles's idea of cognitive assemblage and James Leach's theory of creativity. The article introduces the questions and ideas that drove its conception and emerged during the development and subsequent exhibition of *Double Agent*.

The section History and Theory of Algorithmic Art is opened by the contribution of Patricia de Vries with the title Web Search Fever and Collecting as a Human Condition. De Vries uses the theoretical concepts of the imaginary and Kierkegaard's philosophical discussion of anxiety and relates both to search engines, how we use them, how we imagine what they do and how artists engage with the technology in their art works. Searching is collecting but de Vries also shows that collecting is related to storytelling and leads to narrativization of the collected. Camille Henrot's experimental film *Grosse Fatigue* (2013) has been chosen as it shows how web search can be framed as a form of collecting. De Vries goes one step further and discusses philosophically how collecting can be understood as a human condition.

Angela Krewani's article introduces the relationship between cybernetics and early experiments in computer art. She examines the distinct development paths of cybernetics and computer art in Germany and the United States. She highlights how the discourse surrounding cybernetic art in the United States displayed a welcoming and positive attitude towards the integration of computers into the art field. In contrast, in Germany, a more critical approach is observed. Krewani demonstrates a parallel between this critical stance and the overall German art discourses, which tend to be more sceptical towards technology, mass media, and popular culture.

Anna Luhn explores the application of algorithmic translation techniques in contemporary artistic practice. By examining two specific artworks, namely Baden Pailthorpe's *Lingua Franca* and Julia Nakotte's *#file.read()*, the investigates the role that translation technology may or may not play in the realm of contemporary textual and digital art. She focuses on artworks incorporating machine translation technology and discusses how these artworks can contribute to current reconceptualizations of literary translation.

This special issue closes with a Literature Survey by Mathias Fuchs. Fuchs engages in an endeavour to draw a comparison between two waves of publications focused on algorithmic art. The initial wave of publications spans from 1956 to 1988, while the second wave comprises publications specifically from 2003 to 2021. It is important to note that the selection of texts is not exhaustive and based on the author's personal collection of books on his bookshelves.

References

Benjamin, Walter (1935): L'œuvre d'art à l'époque de sa reproduction mécanisée. In: Zeitschrift für Sozialforschung, Frankfurt: Frankfurter Institut für Sozialforschung.
Bense, Max (1956): Aesthetische Information. Aesthetica II. Krefeld, Baden-Baden: Agis-Verlag.
Bense, Max (1998): "Einführung in die informationsästhetische Ästhetik." In: Max Bense (ed.), Ausgewählte Schriften: Bd. 3: Ästhetik und Texttheorie. Stuttgart: Agis-Verlag, pp. 251–417.
Birkhoff, George D. (1929): Quelques éléments mathématiques de l'art. Bologna: Atti del Congresso Internazionale die Matematici,
Birkhoff, George D. (1931): Une théorie quantitative de l'esthétique. Bulletin de la Société française de Philosophia.
Birkhoff, George D. (1933): Aesthetic Measure. Harvard: Harvard University Press. [cf. Birkhoff's aesthetic measure. https://www.researchgate.net/publication/323296865_Birkhoff's_aesthetic_measure]
Cordeiro, Waldemar (1972): Arteônica. O uso criativo de meios electrônicos nas artes. São Paulo: Universidade de São Paulo.
Kac, Eduardo (2007): Media Poetry: an International Anthology (2nd edition), Bristol: Intellect Books.
Krewani, Angela (2016): Medienkunst: Theorie – Praxis – Ästhetik. Trier: Wissenschaftlicher Verlag.
MacDonald-Korth, D./Lehdonvirta, V./Meyer, E. T. (2018): Art Market 2.0: Blockchain and Financialisation in Visual Arts. London: The Alan Turing Institute.
Moles, Abraham A. (1973): Kunst & Computer. Schauberg, Köln: DuMont.
Nake, Frieder (2012): "Construction and Intuition: Creativity in Early Computer Art." In: McCormack, J.P./ d'Inverno, M. (eds.), Computers and Creativity. Berlin, Heidelberg: JSpringer Verlag
Nake, Frieder (2016): "Die algorithmische Revolution." In: Fuchs-Kittowski, Frank/Kriesel, Werner (eds.), Informatik und Gesellschaft. Festschrift zum 80. Geburtstag von Klaus Fuchs-Kittowski, Frankfurt a. M. u. a.: Peter Lang.
Popper, Frank (1993): Art of the Electronic Age. Greenwich, Connecticut: New York Graphic Society, Ltd,

Reck, Hans Ulrich (2007): The Myth of Media Art. The Aesthetics of the Techno/Imaginary and an Art Theory of Virtual Realities. Weimar: Verlag für Geisteswissenschaften

Zanni, Carlo (2018): Art in the age of the cloud (1st ed.). Milan: Diorama Editions.

Artists' Statements

Artificial Intelligence as Phármakon
Algorithmic Art between Remedy and Poison

Giselle Beiguelman

One of the most disturbing aspects of Artificial Intelligence concerns the anthropocentric spectrum that underlies its concepts and operations. Contrary to the prevailing multi/inter/transspecies thinking dominating the fields of humanities and biological sciences today, from Donna Haraway (2005) and Anna Tsing (2015), through Bruno Latour (1993), Philipe Descola (2010), and Eduardo Viveiros de Castro (2018), it is evident how computation still pursues the paradigm of *Homo sapiens* as the exemplary reference. The vocabulary of AI expresses this dogma, not only in terms of intelligence itself but also in the centrality it attributes to the brain as the exclusive "organ" of intelligence. Many thinkers challenge this thesis, and it is sufficient to mention James Bridle's synthesis in his latest book (*Ways of Being: Animals, Plants, Machines: The Search for a Planetary Intelligence*, 2021). Entirely dedicated to discussing multiple forms of intelligence, especially non-human ones, or, in Bridle's suggested expression, "more than human."

The anthropocentric paradigm underlies all fields of AI and enunciates its colonialist background. Nomenclatures such as neural networks, machine learning, computer vision, natural language processing, self-attention, hallucination, etc., are some examples of this point of view. It is no wonder that it is the cornerstone of current technological disputes, such as Natural Language Processing (NLP), which connects textual language to nature and nature to the human (primarily English-speaking American humans). These foundations extend beyond the field of computer science and also shape our relationship with machines, expecting machines to have a servile vocation in a master/slave mold.

This relationship is consistent with the history of robots since their early days. Ruha Benjamin, one of the most interesting theorists today, draws attention in *Race after Technology* (2019) to how the dynamics of subordination relate to the etymology of the word "robot." In Czech, it means "compulsory labor" and derives from the Slavic "robota," meaning "servitude, deprivation." Ruha shows that robots articulate, through technologies, socially constructed practices of human domination over other humans.

Lucy Schuman, one of the first theorists to discuss interactions between humans and machines in the late 1980s, drew attention to these issues. Truth be told, feminist theorists were pioneers in discussions that transversally addressed technology, patriarchy, colonialism, and capitalism. And how can we forget Donna Haraway's Cyborg Manifesto and her reflections on companion species?

These species inhabit the ecosystem of which humans are also a part and interact in beneficial ways, such as obtaining food, protection, or reproduction. This relational view, which integrates different types of life and other instances, surpasses even the traditional notion of species and encompasses ancestral knowledge about the life of plants.

Companion species also allow us to consider other relationships with machines and their systems. Over the past two years, I have worked extensively with Artificial Intelligence in my artistic projects. It has been a tremendous learning experience. As I am not a programmer, I had to try to understand them, to know their limits and mine. I cannot say that the AIs and I became friends, but we managed to establish partnerships and temporary bonds that re-educated me. Above all, they challenged me to think of machine learning as a pedagogical exercise of attention rather than mere training to accomplish my goals. After all, the gaps between what I wanted to do and the results I achieved were immense (and often more interesting because they surprised me).

Currently, I am exploring natural language-based models that create images from texts and other images in an almost inter-semiotic translation process. The images in this essay were made using this type of programming, employing two complementary methods: text-to-image and image-to-image. They are part of a work in progress, *Poisonous, Noxius, and Suspicious*, a title borrowed from a 19th-century scientific manual. The focus is on plants banned by the colonial "civilizing" process due to their use in sacred rituals and hallucinogenic and aphrodisiac powers, contradicting the canon of the ideal morally and physically superior human (white European man).

Paradoxically, the pharmaceutical industry has reconsidered many condemned plants, appropriating ancestral knowledge about their healing powers (Aronson 2014). In this project, I see them as a kind of *Phármakon*, operating simultaneously as remedy and poison, introducing themselves into the discourse with all their ambivalence (Derrida 1991: 14). All the images have as references women naturalists from the 17th to the 19th centuries, such as Giovanna Grazoni (1600-1670), Maria Sybilla Meriam (1647-1717), Jeanne Baret (1740-1807), Anne Kingsbury Wollstonecraft (1791-1828), Marianne North (1830-1890), Constancia Paca (1844-1920) among others, who have been erased from natural history and art. Because of this, I signed them with their names and the software used to develop the images. It is a distributed process of authorship with all those different companion species (human and non-human). In the captions, I describe the "new" therapeutic uses the pharmaceutical industry nowadays gives those plants.

The entire procedure of creating these images involves several successive operations, in which an image created by text, through descriptions that feed the NLP, is then "polished," using this first image as input for the AI to be remade by other authors, taking advantage of its resources. The biggest challenge is dealing with algorithmic censorship, something I have experienced since *Botannica Tirannica* (2022), in which I worked with plants with anti-Semitic, racist, and misogynistic names (both common and scientific), generating new beings beyond the traditional animal, vegetal, mineral domains. Since I work on these projects with sensitive words and terms, referring to gender, race, religion, and now with plants related to drugs and forbidden substances, most native to the tropics, the program constantly blocks me. I have developed a series of tactical expedients to discuss species with botanical nomenclature with prejudiced names and androgynous beings, using scientific terminology and Latin names.

Throughout the working process, I often recalled my friend Eduardo Kac, an artist and professor at the Chicago Art Institute, a pioneer of cybernetic art, explaining to me the importance of the chess match between Garry Kasparov and the IBM supercomputer Deep Blue in which the famous Russian chess player was defeated on the 36th move. At that moment, the machine exhibited subtlety, and Kasparov lost because he followed the game's rules. This event inspired Kac's work "Move 36" and was an impulse for my research.

The lessons from that match are not, as IBM marketing possibly intended, to prove the superiority of the machine over the human. Instead, they demonstrate that Artificial Intelligence implies another paradigm of knowledge. This paradigm requires us to disregard Homo erectus and seek the Homo multitudes, as Haraway speaks of, with all its ancestries, multiple genders, and parallel relatives.

Within this spectrum of questions, I encountered NLP in a kind of Talmudic experience, where every question must be answered with another. I understood Derrida's meaning that it is necessary to close the book to open the text. Opening the text to the diversity of subjects that write it provides more room for suspension than suspicion. In other words, opening the text through the arts of companionship. Companionship worldviews indicate that breaking with anthropocentrism presupposes learning to unlearn.

This perspective also involves thinking about technology beyond the role of an obedient tool, as a co-pilot or virtual assistant, terms as simplistic as the market that produces them. These ambitions are limited to desiring a generation of "Robot sapiens" and betting, once again, on the future of the past. How can we design machines as otherness and not as expanded versions of ourselves? How can we create companion machines? Do current popular resources like ChatGPT and Midjourney point to these possibilities?

I believe not. They are products already packaged with a series of problems, such as market pressure that forces their release before they are ready, and that tends to worsen with the war between Google and Microsoft for control of "natural language" search. However, as a system, I believe so. Because it allows us to desire relational machines in a world that, after the dissemination of Artificial Intelligence NLP-based technologies, is no longer the same.

References

Aronson, J. K. (2014): "Plant Poisons and Traditional Medicines. In: J. Farrar, P. J. Hotez, T. Junghanss, G. Kang, D. Lalloo, & N. J. White (Eds.), *Manson's Tropical Infectious Diseases* (23rd Edition) (p. 1128-1150.e6). W.B. Saunders. https://doi.org/10.1016/B978-0-7020-5101-2.00077-7.

Beiguelman, G. (2022): *Botannica Tirannica*. Botannica Tirannica. https://botanicatirannica.desvirtual.com/

Benjamin, R. (2019): *Race After Technology: Abolitionist Tools for the New Jim Code*. Polity.

Bridle, J. (2023 [2021]): *Maneiras de ser: Animais, plantas, máquinas: a busca por uma inteligência planetária*. Todavia.

Castro, E. V. de. (2018): *Metafísicas canibais: Elementos para uma antropolia pós-estrutural* (1ª edição). Ubu Editora.

Derrida, J. (1973 [1967]) : *Gramatologia*. Perspectiva.

Derrida, J. (1991 [1972]): *A Farmácia de Platão*. Iluminuras.

Descola, P., & Ciscato, C. (2016 [2010]): *Outras naturezas, outras culturas*. Editora 34.

Haraway, D. J. (2005): *The Companion Species Manifesto: Dogs, People, and Significant Otherness*. Prickly Paradigm Press.

Kac, E. (2004): *MOVE 36*. https://www.ekac.org/move36.html

Latour, B. (2019 [1993]): *Jamais fomos modernos: Ensaio de antropologia simétrica* . Editora 34.

Pratt, A. (1857): *Poisonous, noxious, and suspected plants, of our fields and woods*. Society for Promoting Christian Knowledge. https://www.biodiversitylibrary.org/item/258098

Suchman, L. (2006): *Human-Machine Reconfigurations: Plans and Situated Actions* (2nd ed). Cambridge University Press.

Tsing, A. L. (2021 [2015]): *The Mushroom at the End of the World: On the Possibility of Life in Capitalist Ruins*. Princeton University Press.

Fig. 1: A grove of Ipomoea tricolor (Morning-glory) flowers and Lophophora williamsii (Peyotl), 1850. Marianne North+Giselle Beiguelman+DALLE2+Runway. From the series: Poisonous, Noxious, and Suspected (2023).
Considered hallucinogens, both have substances associated with therapeutic uses for mental disorders and different body pains

Fig.2: field, by the sea, full of Cannabis sativa with many Papaver somniferum (poppies), and Catharanthus rose (Madagascar periwinkles) in a forest of Physostigma venenosum (Calabar beans). Giovana Grazosi+Giselle Beiguelman+DALLE2+Runway. From the series: Poisonous, Noxious, and Suspected (2023).
These plants have therapeutic agents used in palliative care, analgesics, and muscle fatigue

Fig. 3: A forest of giant Nepenthes northiana (Monkey cup) by Marianne North, 1810. From the series: Poisonous, Noxious, and Suspected (2023).
Popularly named "carnivorous plants", by feeding on mosquitoes, these plants populated the collective imagination of the colonizers with monstrous figures that supposedly inhabited the forests of the tropics

Fig. 4: Pilocarpus jaborandi in a rain forest, 1825. Maria Graham +Giselle Beiguelman+DALLE2+Runway. From the series: Poisonous, Noxious, and Suspected (2023).
Extracted from jaborandi, Pilocarpine is a substance used to treat glaucoma.

Artificial Intelligence as Phármakon 23

Fig. 5: Iboga and Camptotheca acuminata (Cancer trees) with indigenous people in healing rituals. Jeanne Baret +Giselle Beiguelman+DALLE2+Runway. From the series: Poisonous, Noxious, and Suspected (2023).
This tree, considered dangerous for decades, produces inhibitors that are being studied as potential medicine components for curing certain types of cancer.

Fig. 6: Poisonous mushrooms with flower buds of Mandragoras, 1910. Constancia Peca+Giselle Beiguelman+DALLE2+Runway. From the series: Poisonous, Noxious, and Suspected (2023).
Nazi propaganda referred to Jews as Der Giftpilz (poisonous mushroom). Mandragora, native to South Africa, is a ritualistic plant among various ancient peoples and continues to be erroneously associated with black magic due to colonialist influences.

Impressionistic Programming
Aesthetical and technical methods for creating the interactive artwork "Portrait on the Fly"

Laurent Mignonneau and Christa Sommerer

Abstract

This article describes our artistic practice of creating algorithmic art with a special focus on interactive computer installations that model natural processes and involve the public into the creation of art. We demonstrate how we created one of our interactive installations, "Portrait on the Fly". It was conceived and realized using observation and nature studies. We will explain how the programming and coding was undertaken. We will also illustrate our method of abstracting natural phenomena through what we call the "Impressionistic Programming" approach.

Keywords

Generative Art, Artificial Life Art, Interactive Art, Impressionistic Programming

Introduction

Throughout the last 30 years we have been creating interactive artworks that are inspired by natural phenomena. We are considered one of the forerunners of interactive art and in particular *Generative Art* and *Artificial Life Art*. We design our artworks as open systems, where the user input leads to dynamic, non-predictable and open-ended visual results. Creating virtual worlds on a computer and letting users interact with these virtual worlds through intuitive or multi-modal interfaces allows us to create artworks that are dynamically changing and never pre-defined. They are rather co-created by the users and co-evolve through the interaction of the users with the system, i.e. the algorithms implemented via our software (Sommerer/Mignonneau 1998: 148-161). In our recent retrospective exhibition "The Artwork as a Living System" (Sommerer/Mignonneau 2022), we present around 15 artworks that use these principles and methods. All these artworks are described in the monograph "Christa Sommerer & Laurent Mignonneau: The Artwork as a Living System" published by MIT Press' Leonardo book series. (Ohlenschläger/Weibel/Weidinger 2022)

The retrospective exhibition also provides a good occasion to recapitulate some of the programming methods we have developed over the past 30 years. In 2006 we published "From the Poesy of Programming to Research as Art Form" (Mignonneau/Sommerer 2006). In the paper we stated "[a]s media artists we have chosen to become artists/researchers or researcher/artists who define and shape new questions of creation, and set-out to explore the fore-front of creativity and digital technology, investigating the very question of creation, invention and discovery." (ibid: 170) What we meant back then was that programming itself can be an act of artistic creation, even though it might appear purely mathematical and technical at first glance.

We are not alone in pointing out the close relationship of programming and creativity. From the 1960s on early pioneers of computer art, such as Georg Nees, Frieder Nake, Charles Csuri, Vera Molnar, Manfred Mohr and others have already investigated how computer software can be used for artistic and aesthetic purposes. These artists have been called the "algorists", as they investigated computer algorithms for art making. Frieder Nake describes the *algorists* as "artists of a new kind: they *think* their works and let machines carry them out. These artists live between aesthetics and algorithms and, insofar, they constitute a genuinely new species. They do art in postmodern times." (Nake 2012: 65)

In the same article, Frieder Nake describes this new relationship between the artist and the machine as a change in attitude. When artists decide to use algorithms and "semiotic machines" this is much more than just using the computer as a tool. Nake claims that the change is "characterized by explicitness, computability, distance, decontextualiization, semioticity." These changes provide a huge potential to the artists' creative capacities but Nake doesn't go so far as to call the computer itself creative (ibid: 93).

Nake analyses how writing computer programs impacts the artist´s creativity. He says: "The creation of a work that may become a work of art may be seen as changing the state of some material in such a way that an idea or intent takes on shape. The material sets its resistance against the artist´s will to form. Creativity in the artistic domain is, therefore, determined by overcoming and breaking the material´s resistance. If this is accepted, the question arises what, in the case of algorithmic art, takes on the role of resistant material. The resistant material is clearly the algorithm. It needs to be formed such that it is then ready to perform in the way the artist wants it to do". (ibid)

Other artists have also described the creative and aesthetic potential of computer programs. The Austrian pioneer of computer art, Herbert W. Franke, wrote in 1985: "'Free' computer graphics can serve as a source of new programming methods and of ideas for creating new shapes. It is through playful experiments, but also through confrontation with classical art, that experience is gained which can be useful in several ways." (Nake 2012: 93)

Paul Fishwick's *Aesthetic Computing* (2006) points out the relationship of programming, art and aesthetics. In his edited volume important practitioners describe their methods and principles when creating computer art or computer-aided visualizations. Donna Cox demonstrates how scientific visualizations (data-viz) transform numerical data into digital visual models (visaphors) via processes of creative mapping. She writes: "Likewise, data-viz is a mapping process from numbers into pictures that results in visaphors, a digital visual metaphor.... however, the primary focus here is on the creation of visaphors in the art of visualization and the relationship to contemporary Metaphor Theory." (Cox 2006: 89) Cox stresses that Metaphor Theory is useful here as it is "looking at cognitive process of understanding one domain of information in terms of another domain of information ... The process of mapping is important to understanding how metaphors create new meaning and how this mapping relates to data-viz." (ibid: 90-91)

The media artists Monika Fleischmann and Wolfgang Strauss highlight the relationship between computing and art and the necessary transformation and mapping process: "In this way the concept of visualization familiar to computer science is put into a sensory and cognitive context, for, after all, an important role of media art is to show how we understand what we see and perceive." (Fleischmann/Strauss 2006: 115)

Let us now see how we, within our own art practice, deal with what Nake called the *resistance of the algorithm* and its explicitness, and how we can introduce artistic qualities, poetry and metaphors into our interactive art projects.

Case Study: Portrait on the Fly—Impressionist Programming

Since 30 years Laurent Mignonneau has refined his method of creating interactive artworks, by on the one hand studying phenomena of nature and on the other hand creating computer algorithms and hardware interfaces to recreate those phenomena for new experiences in media art. Over the years a specific method has emerged that we could call the "Impressionistic Programming" method. In the following case study, we will describe one of our artworks in more detail and illustrate what we mean by this.

Portrait on the Fly

From around 2006 on we became interested in studying flies and how they move. The initial inspiration came from observing flies in our winter garden. Once the flies entered by the terrace door, many of them would be trapped in the winter garden room and it was hard for them to find their way out, even though the door was left open. Many actions to catch them and chase them out were unsuccessful. The flies would stubbornly swarm around or stick to a window until they were completely exhausted. Most of the time they would die after a day or two, desperately struggling to find a way out. Our efforts to rescue them failed in most of the cases. We felt really bad about having so many dead flies in our winter garden, and therefore decided to create an artwork in honour of them. We started to observe them more closely and especially looked at their flying behaviour. We could see that they have a rather complex way of moving around, but mostly sought for bright areas. This is why they did not conceive the open door as a potential exit. We then started making sketches of insects and of the corresponding flying patterns (Fig. 1).

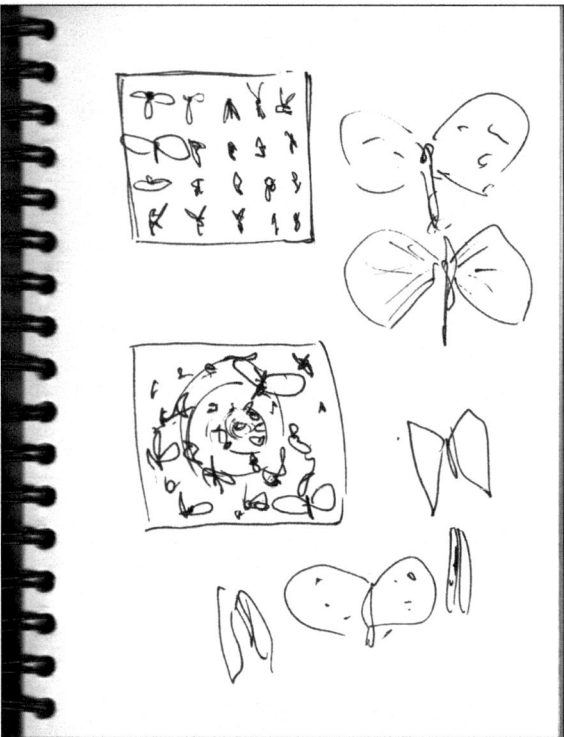

Fig. 1: Studies of flies and their flying pattern, 2007.

When pondering upon the question of the relationship between humans and flies we realized that most people do not like these insects, as they can be quite annoying. In fact, in many cultures the image of a fly is associated with death and decay as flies often infest dead bodies. In forensic entomology, for example, the development stage of the fly larvae is used to determine the exact time of death of a human or animal corpse. Besides this rather macabre fact, we also found out that the motif of the fly in art history was often used to symbolize death and decay and to remind the viewer of life´s brevity (Chastel 1984). A special genre of still life paintings, called vanitas, frequently depicts plants, fruits and insects, and this has been popular in the 16th and 17th century. A great example are the works by **Abraham Mignon** (Kraemer-Noble 2008).

Fig. 2: Abraham Mignon, Still life with peonies, roses, parrot tulips, morning glory, an iris and poppies in a glass vase set within a stone niche and caterpillars, a snail, a bee and a cockchafer on the ledge below, around 1670, oil on canvas, 60.5 cm x 50.9 cm.

Around 2007, that is the time when we started studying flies, we also finished an artwork called *Wissensgewächs* (Sommerer/Mignonneau 2022: 202-205). It was first shown as a large-scale interactive media facade with 16 interactive screens at the City of Science in Braunschweig and later in a one screen version at the "Open Space" exhibition at the NTT-ICC museum in Tokyo in 2008. In this interactive installation people could walk in front of an interactive screen and see their own portrait composed from various generative plant types, as shown in Figure 3.

The main inspiration for the piece came from our fascination for Arcimboldo's 16th century organic portraits that are composed out of plant and animal motives (Ferino-Padgen 2007: 19), as shown in Figure 4.

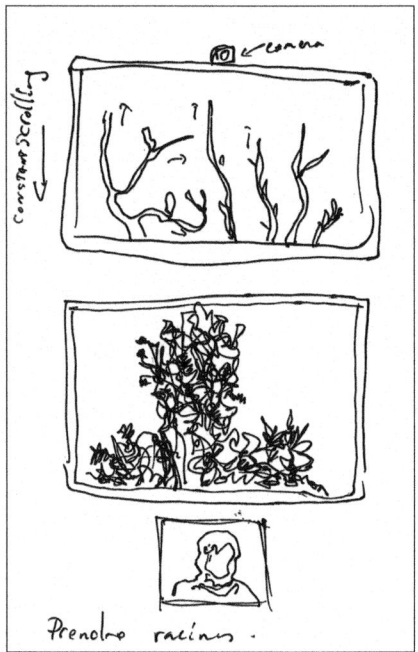

Fig. 3: Wissensgewächs, an interactive portrait composed of plant motives, sketch for the interactive installation, Braunschweig, 2006.

Fig. 4: Giuseppe Arcimboldo: Summer, 1563.

Finally, inspired by Arcimboldo and by our studies of flies, we saw the potential of creating interactive portraits. This is how the idea for *Portrait on the Fly* emerged. Laurent created a first sketch for the interactive installation in 2007, shown in Figure 5.

Fig. 5: *Portrait on the Fly*—interactive installation, initial sketch, 2007.

The conceptual idea for *Portrait on the Fly* was that people would walk in front of a large monitor with a video camera attached to the top of it and they would suddenly see a portrait of themselves composed of a large swarm of flies, as sketched in Figure 6.

Laurent started to use his observations of the flying patterns of flies to write a computer program in C++ that simulates the flying behaviour of an individual fly. After several tests, Laurent decided to not create a 3D fly but instead use a top view photograph of a real fly. We kept the 3D model of flies for two of our later VR works, called *Flies in the Sky* (2017) and *Fly Simulator* (2018). We also decided to reduce the complexity of the flying pattern. The artificial fly walks in 2D space on an invisible glass window. The actual flying behaviour was, however, implemented for the piece *People on the Fly* which we finished in 2016. In *Portrait on the Fly* the fly moves randomly and can never pass the border of the virtual glass window, i.e. the screen borders. Imagine this as if a natural insect would be constrained by a windowpane.

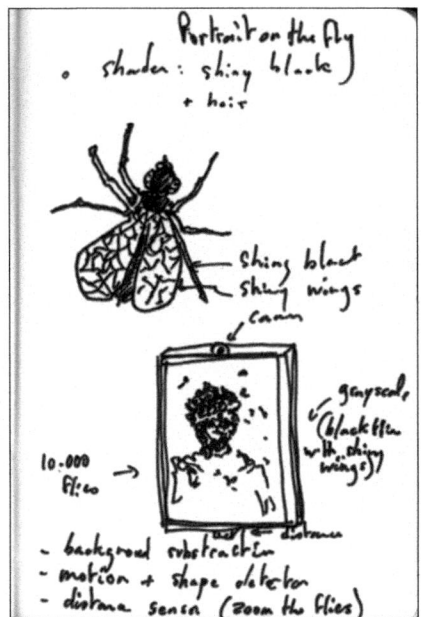

Fig. 6: *Portrait on the Fly*—interactive installation, early sketch, 2008.

The algorithm Laurent created is based on one single rule: each virtual fly moves randomly until the pixel brightness value[1] of the video images it walks upon changes massively. In this case the virtual insect would stop walking and wait for the pixel brightness value at its position going back to the previous value. By spawning 10,000 virtual flies behaving this way, a silhouette becomes visible whenever a person enters the camera's field of view.

Instead of modelling a very complex swarm of flies, the single rule algorithm creates a pointillist contour of the visitor. The emerging shapes are easily recognizable by the visitor as their own contour shapes, despite a high level of abstraction.

The individual fly does not track contours of a visitor. It is rather the high number of flies that creates the impression of an organized insect swarm mimicking the contours of a visitor as shown in Figure 7.

---

1   In terms of algorithm the entire picture frame content is in grayscale, the brightness value of a certain pixel at the fly's position is compared to the pixel brightness value where the fly is going to be next. An action is taken if the difference between the two values exceeds a given threshold value. The fly will therefore walk if the difference is kept low and stop walking as soon as the difference is higher than the threshold.

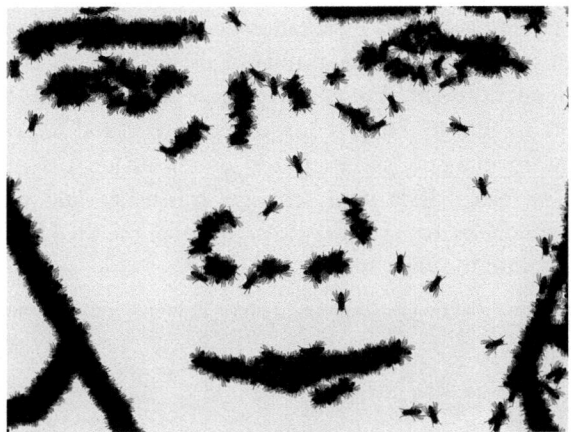

Fig. 7: Portrait on the Fly software—lines appearing from flies that sit down when they detect a pixel brightness value change in the live feed of the camera.

A portrait that is created through several thousand flies is shown in Figure 8.

Fig. 8: Portrait in the Fly—A user creating his fly portrait by standing in front of the screen.

Visitors to the *Portrait on the Fly* installation can thus see a line portrait of themselves emerging out of tens of thousands of digital flies on display. Even the slightest movement of the head or of any parts of the visitor's body chases them off. The portraits are thus in constant flux, they construct and deconstruct. *Portrait on the Fly* is a commentary on "selfie culture", our obsession with making pictures of ourselves. The piece deals with "change, transience and impermanence." (Sommerer/Mignonneau 2022: 244-251) An image of the final installation where a visitor interacts with the work is shown in Figure 9.

Fig. 9: *Portrait on the Fly* interactive installation at the Artists et Robot exhibition, Grand Palais, Paris, 2018.

During the development of the software, Laurent remarked how much we, as users, can contribute to the reconstruction of a full image from a partial image, when looking at it. He also found out that staying immobile in front of a camera is not as easy as it seems. Some visitors would not see their contour being formed by flies as these visitors were constantly moving in front of the screen. One can, however, only understand the piece's inherent functions when pausing in front of the screen.

Rather than trying to reconstruct a real fly's behaviour, Laurent programmed the impressions we have when watching swarm movements. By accumulating a large number of flies on the screen, the sensation of an uncontrollable mass of insects was created, where one would not anymore be able to follow the movement of a single fly. The quick state change of each fly in the programme reflects the amazing rapidity of real flies, as they are very fast to evaluate any movement in their immediate environment, taking action in an instant.

When we presented the *Portrait on the Fly* installation a common comment by the visitors was that they believed that real flies would be modelled and that these flies looked very realistic to them. This showed us that even with a rather simple algorithm a realistic impression of a fly´s flying behaviour could be created.

What is Impressionist Programming?

As described above, we came to the idea of calling this programming approach "impressionist programming." What we mean by this, is that instead of trying to exactly imitate the flying pattern of the fly, or even its realistic look, we use a simplified technique that only gives the impression as if it was moving naturally. We take this approach from *Impressionism* (Broude 1994), an artistic movement from the 19th century, where artists such as Monet and others created paintings of nature that give overall natural visual effects instead of showing all the details. Monet described his creation process as follows: "All I know is that I do what I can to represent what nature makes me feel, and more often than not, in trying to represent what I feel, I totally forget the most elementary rules of painting, if indeed there are any. In short, in the effort to capture my sensations, I allow many mistakes to appear." (Pagé 2022: 18) In fact when standing in front of one of Monet´s famous *Nymphéas* (1897-1926), one can feel the sensation Monet must have had when looking at the beautiful pond with its water lilies and reflections trough the water (21). The use of broken brush strokes and the clever mix of colours only give us the visual impression of the plants and the water, without actually being able to depict any exact details. It is in the eyes of the viewers that the picture is completed and the impression of seeing nature is created.

Conclusion

To summarize we can say that in the past years we have been developing a creation and programming method that is based on a method that can be considered similar to the painting practice of the Impressionists. Instead of an exact reproduction of nature or an imitation of natural phenomena, we try to model the impression that nature has on us. Not unlike what Claude Monet did for painting, we are as media artists interested in the feelings we have when looking at insects, plants or landscapes. We try to represent those feelings by making artificial insects fly and swarm around, or by creating virtual plants grow in an interactive digital garden. (Ohlenschläger/Weibel/Weidinger 2022) While computing is tied to computability, prediction and certainty, we agree with Monet about the importance of mistakes, intuition, imprecisions and impressions. We absolutely agree with the before mentioned Frieder Nake, that in computer art intuition is important and necessary: "Construction, we may be inclined to say, can systematically be controlled; intuition, in comparison emerges and happens in uncontrolled ways. Construction stands for the systematic aspects of works we do; intuition for the immediate, non-considerate, and spontaneous. Both are necessary for creation." (Nake 2012: 92) To sum up we can say that various artists in the field of computer art have pointed out a need for an intentional lack of sharpness, metaphors and intuition and we may add our *Impressionistic Programming* method to this discourse.

References

Broude, N. (1994): World Impressionism, Harry N. Abrams.
Chastel, A. (1984): Musca Depicta, Franco Maria Ricci Editore, Fontanellato.
Cox, D. (2006): "Metaphoric Mappings: The Art of Visualization." In: Fishwick, P. (Ed.), Aesthetic Computing, Cambridge, MA: MIT Press.
Ferino-Padgen, S. (2007): Giuseppe Arcimboldo: Court Artist, Philosopher, Rhétoriqueur, Magician or an Entertainer? Arcimboldo 1526-1593, Skira Editore and Kunsthistorisches Museum Wien.
Fishwick, P. (2006): Aesthetic Computing, Cambridge, MA: MIT Press.
Fleischmann M./Strauss, W. (2006): Public "Public Space of Knowledge – Artistic Practice" In: Fishwick, P. (ed.), Aesthetic Computing, Cambridge, MA: MIT Press.
Franke, H. W. (1985): "The New Visual Age: The Influence of Computer Graphics on Art and Society." In: *Leonardo* 18/2
Kraemer-Noble, Magdalena (2007): Abraham Mignon 1640-1679. Michael Imhof, Petersberg.
Mignonneau, L./Sommerer, C. (2006): "From the Poesy of Programming to Research as Art Form." In: Fishwick, P. (Ed.), Aesthetic Computing, Cambridge, MA: MIT Press.
Monet, C. (1912): Letter of June 7, 1912 to Gustave Geffroy.
Monet, C. (1916-1919): "Nymphéas, Oil on canvas 200 x 180 cm, Paris, Musée Marmottan Monet." In: Monet Mitchel, Foundation Louis Vuitton and Musée Marmottan Monet.
Nake, F. (2012): "Construction and Intuition: Creativity in Early Computer Art." In: McCormack, J./d'Inverno, M. (Eds.), *Computers and Creativity*, Berlin, Heidelberg: Springer Verlag.
Ohlenschläger, K./Weibel, P./Weidinger, A. (2022): Christa Sommerer & Laurent Mignonneau: The Artwork as a Living System, Leonardo Book Series, MIT Press.
Sommerer, C./Mignonneau, L. (1998): Art as A Living System, In: Art @ Sciences, Springer Verlag, Vienna and New York.

Sommerer, C./Mignonneau, L. (2007): "Wissensgewächs—a growing media facade that reflects the visitor´s attention and interest'" In: Ohlenschläger, K./Weibel, P./Weidinger, A.: Christa Sommerer & Laurent Mignonneau.A. Leonardo Book Series, Boston: MIT Press..

Sommerer, C./Mignonneau, L. (2022): The Artwork as a Living System, Retrospective exhibition at the ZMK Karlsruhe, 7.5.-31.7.2022, https://zkm.de/en/exhibition/2022/05/christa-sommerer-laurent-mignonneau-the-artwork-as-a-living-system (last accessed 16.12.2022)

Wildenstein, D. (2022): "Giverny. Catalogue Raisonné, vol. IV, letter no. 2015." quoted in: Suzanne Pagé, Listening to the artworks, In: Monet-Mitchell, Foundation Louis Vuitton and Musée Marmottan Monet.

Against the Norm
Othering and Otherness in AI Aesthetics

Marco Donnarumma

Abstract

What are the links between science, aesthetics and episteme sustaining the large deep learning models known as AI image generators, such as Dall-e, StableDiffusion and Midjourney? Here I argue that these software systems are an expression of the normative power wielded by the industrial-cultural complex that funds, produces and disseminates them. This form of expression is what I call corporate AI aesthetics or, in short, AI aesthetics. My argumentation begins by defining the particular kind of aesthetics that AI image generators yield and then journeys through the enforcement of neoliberal knowledge they contribute to. Through the lens of cultural criticism and anticolonial scholarship, I try to develop a critique of AI aesthetics as soft propaganda for the Global North. In this sense, AI aesthetics disseminates a techno-deterministic view where anything that is or can be made countable, like human creativity, can be predicted, hence, controlled. To this end, I discuss the cultural and technical production of AI artefacts, emphasising its dependence on an abstraction of labour, the reinforcement of biases in visual culture and the deceit of art market speculations. The discussion leads to observe what AI aesthetics detracts attention from: an understanding of artistic intention as a form of collective otherness; that is, artistic intention not as the will of an inspired individual or a powerful AI system, but as the flow of relations among human and non-humans, existing across generations, cultures and geographies. Such a relational ecosystem becomes manifest in the analysis of two artworks, by Jonathan Chaim Reus and artist group Electrobiota, that are representative of an affirmative, critical and culturally situated approach to deep learning.

Keywords

AI art, aesthetics, capitalism and art market, deep learning, othering, otherness

1. Aesthetics of Power

This text is concerned with an analysis of some components of what I call *corporate AI aesthetics*. For brevity and clarity, I will refer to it as AI aesthetics. This is a widespread and dominating visual aesthetics that has been popularised by the major players in the artificial intelligence and deep learning business, US-based corporations Google, Nvidia, Meta, OpenAI, and more recently by smaller actors, such as the US company Midjourney and the British Stability AI[1]. AI aesthetics is highly recognizable and lies at the core of what some identify as 'AI Art', the production of images by means of very large algorithmic systems, called AI image generators. Many generators exists today, but their core theory and implementation is tied to a handful of corporate and independent organizations with access to large financial and computational resources, sometimes in collaboration with university research groups that receive funds from them. Here, my focus will be on what kind of artistic expression AI aesthetics yields and how that expression exists in relation with complexes of what turns out to be normative power. In order to tackle these questions, I will discuss how AI aesthetic is produced technically *and* culturally. This will mean situating the technical operations of AI image generators within the cultural-industrial milieu where they thrive: an assemblage of industry business plans, art market operations and technocratic ideologies that, through deep learning, produces a particular type of reality. I will refer to this milieu as the *AI complex*.

Why the need to link aesthetics and power? Some may argue that deep learning is a technological breakthrough and AI art is proof of the novelty of such a computational paradigm. Others would argue that deep learning image generators may be a lightning trend, fated to fade out of public view (just like other unfortunate inventions) or to transmogrify into commercial video plug-ins. I in part agree with both views. Yet, a careful look reveals a more complex picture: from profiling, microtargeting, media recommendation and predictive policing to finance, climate modelling, autonomous weapons and art, deep and probabilistic learning technologies have come to structure and sustain contemporary capitalist societies. While they also made possible important technological breakthroughs, for example in the study of climate change and biodiversity loss, the widespread adoption of deep learning across disciplines has accelerated a drastic societal change. It has materialised in a technocratic ideology of prediction as a scaffold of political, social, moral and cultural life. By looking at the controversies surrounding deep learning and prediction methods it shall be evident how problematic and dangerous this approach can be; think of the role of Cambridge

---

1   Midjourney is owned by David Holz, a Silicon Valley entrepreneur who previously headed the Leap Motion technology startup. Stability AI is owned by Emad Mostaque, a hedge fund manager.

Analytica in both the Leave.EU campaign for Brexit (UK Parliament 2022) and the Trump US election campaign in 2016 (Hu 2020); the entanglement of US military and Google in Project Maven, where Google's machine learning library, TensorFlow, was used to enhance warfare drones and analyse surveillance data (Hoijtink/Planqué-Van Hardeveld 2022); the capacity of forecasting algorithms and agent-based systems to destabilise already volatile financial markets—which became apparent in the flash crash of 2010 (Sornette/Von der Becke 2011: 15) and is still being debated since then (Blyth 2018; Olorunnimbe/Viktor 2022); the automated exploitation of labour from Amazon and Netflix to Uber, Spotify and Airbnb (Casilli/Posada 2019); and the negative, even deadly, psychological impact of Meta's Instagram on children (Yearwood 2022; Milmo 2022). Acknowledging AI art as deeply embedded in the ramified, capital-driven regime of deep learning begs the question: what relation exists between the aesthetics of deep learning imagery and the techno-deterministic drive of the AI complex?

The AI complex can be understood as an intricate configuration of different powers; it entangles corporations, rich individuals, universities, governments, culture and people in interacting feedback loops. The AI complex does not only create technologies; it engineers platforms to deploy those technologies and then enthrals users to inhabit them. Platforms have rules, encourage particular ways of being and modes of understanding. Because these loops involve large networks of people, what emerges is the normalization of one particular world view and the obfuscation of those differing from it. What becomes normalized is a view that posits probabilistic computation and the platforms through which it inhabits the world as key to predict—hence, control—any type of phenomena, from elections to shopping and from self-image to creativity. Deep learning and Big Data are instrumental to the process. In this article, I argue that the very functioning of AI art generators is determined by the power dynamics of the AI complex and, therefore, the kind of aesthetics that AI art expresses is submitted to those powers. Ultimately, it *is* an expression of those powers. Thinking, with Sylvia Wynter (2015), about the link of science, aesthetics and episteme: as long as these types of AI systems remain bound to the AI complex, the aesthetics they afford will continue enacting a sublimation of the current order of knowledge, an order necessary to the "present neoliberal/neo-imperial [...] global order of worlds and things" (ibid: 30). I will come back to this in the penultimate section of the article.

It should be noted that I write this text from the perspective of a media and performance artist, programmer and scholar who has worked with AI, among other technologies, for the last ten years of his career, usually in collaboration with scientists and research laboratories and always with open source systems[2]. I do not despise AI technologies - quite on the contrary, I am continuously intrigued by their aesthetic and epistemic potential (Caramiaux/Donnarumma 2021). My

---

2   My artworks can be viewed at https://marcodonnarumma.com.

critique harbours, at its core, an affirmative wish for AI technologies and their cultural instantiations to be increasingly and critically shaped by artists. It is my hope that by contemplating the links between aesthetics and power in AI art, I can formulate that objective with a stimulating sense of urgency. The critique that follows is, therefore, not directly addressed at artists, users or researchers. Many artists currently use deep learning tools, and the aesthetics of their work range widely in terms of quality and expression. An enquiry into those works would require a different framing from the one I adopt here. In closing the article, I will, however, enter into a generative dialogue with two particular artworks that I see representative of an affirmative, critical and culturally situated approach to deep learning. This dialogue will show some ways in which artistic uses of deep learning can encourage artists and public to explore alternative ways of thinking about artificial intelligence, ways that discard capital-driven norms of creativity and thus question the operating modes and platforms of the AI complex. To release such potential, I suggest, these technologies should be used according to an old tenet of media art practice that seems to have lost currency lately: to 'pervert technological correctness' (Lozano-Hemmer 1996), that is, to enact interventions within the guts of a machine, to creatively feed on criticism about technological novelty, speed and beauty and to turn technological limits and flaws into aesthetic strategies.

2. AI is not a Thing

Before diving into my enquiry, it is helpful to clarify some issues of terminology and navigate a brief historical overview of the field. Today's most advanced AI systems are still far from achieving a general intelligence. In this sense, AI is less a definite concept fully manifested in a machine and more a general idiom that signifies many things at once according to the context where it is spoken. The most precise way to think of AI is as a discipline of study focusing on how machines, software and hardware, can 'learn' particular tasks. Despite its ubiquity, the term 'learning' is strictly a euphemism; a machine does not learn in the conventional sense of the term, it does not craft a skill *and* gather transferable knowledge by being embedded in the world and in relation with others[3]. An AI system finds recurrent patterns in data, which allows it to classify items according to categories or to map the image of a dog to a label that reads 'dog'. Rather than learning, a more appropriate term would be pattern matching, feature mapping or data averaging.

---

3   It should be noted that research on reinforcement learning for robotics often focus on robots' 'learning' in an environment or in partnership with a human. While several successful case studies exist, the results are incomparable to the behavioural plasticity of an animal.

This leads us to another issue of terminology, the very label artificial intelligence. This, arguably, is an ill-chosen name, for it is haunted by the reductionist and anthropocentric notion of intelligence that was predominant in the 1950s, when the term began being used (McCarthy et al. 1955). Today, thanks to a broader and interdisciplinary scope, scientific understanding of intelligence provides insight into the varied forms in which it is manifested across plants, trees, insects, invertebrates and other living beings. While the Western use of the idiom 'AI' is largely still alien to this knowledge, Indigenous epistemologies offer serious alternate perspectives (Lewis et al. 2018).

The arguably reductionist understanding of intelligence at the core of much AI research can be traced along its two main study traditions: "the logic-inspired and the neural-network-inspired paradigms for cognition" (Lecun et al. 2015: 441), also known as, respectively, symbolic and connectionist approach. Each approach represents a different way of understanding how human intelligence works (Smolensky 1987) and both largely neglect the role of embodiment in the process of learning. Symbolic AI is the classical approach and posits that humans make intelligent decisions by manipulating symbols through logic, for example: *If COLD OUTSIDE then WEAR COAT.* Symbolic AI uses large, linear sequences of logic operations to manipulate a pre-known set of symbols, and can, therefore, excel at logical inference and description as long as its field of action is precisely defined. The symbolic approach also proves to be too coarse and rigid when applied to computation with fuzzy data or unknown variables. Here, knowledge is enshrined in symbols and there is a limit to how many symbols a system can handle, especially since a symbol lacks an internal informational structure that defines its features. Once considered the best approach to reconstructing human-like intelligence, with time, research on symbolic AI lost its appeal. A particular thorny problem for researchers was that it could not fully explain how the material construction of the brain, its neurons and networks, scales up to a symbol management system.

This question was more successfully addressed by the connectionist approach. This method is directly inspired by the material arrangement of animal neural networks and their multithreaded mode of operation. That is, a neuron performs a simple and small operation, but it does so in unison with other million neurons, as part of a network where they are all connected to one another. According to the connectionist school of thought, within such a system—be it living or machinic—inference happens not through logic, but through statistical operations. For Lecun et al. (2015: 441) this is a form of "fast 'intuitive' inference that underpins effortless common sense reasoning." Such cognitive model can be represented as a non-linear system where a rational choice emerges from the multiple, simultaneous operation of groups of neurons. They do not hold intelligence in themselves, it is their number and their statistical relations that allow data to be manipulated from a granular level up to higher scales that eventually yield an intelligent decision. Artificial neural networks are systems that attempt to approximate the human brain from a strictly connectionist point of view. As such, they require a vast amount of computational power and data. For this reason, research on neural networks was abandoned in the mid 1970s, and for the same reason it was revived around 2012 by corporations such as Google, Microsoft, Amazon and Meta in the US (Sudmann 2018) and Baidu (Kai 2013) and Tencent in China (Zou 2014). Data and computational power are, in fact, their monopoly.

The symbolic and connectionist approaches generated an innumerable amount of algorithmic techniques that can be broadly grouped into supervised, unsupervised and semisupervised learning, reinforcement learning, ensemble learning, instance-based learning and neural networks. Deep learning and probabilistic learning rely on a connectionist approach, yet may borrow components from a diverse range of techniques. The two methods are interrelated and lie at the core of so called AI image generators. In my view, this is another misnomer, for, as we will see in the next section, these AI systems operate more like filters than generators. They use gargantuan neural networks containing billions of artificial neurons and parameters to guide filtering of visual noise[4] in the shape of a coherent image. Because they follow the principles of the connectionist approach they are void of symbolic logic, manipulate numerical variables instead of symbols and excel at statistical inference from gigantic datasets. This also means that their functioning eschews a scientific ground truth or an established set of concepts. Rather, they *find* meaning within data. Establishing whether that meaning is truthful or useful is an unwelcome responsibility for those who own and use the systems. As a result, deep learning research lives in the shadow of the black-box issue, a serious problem of interpretability and ethics afflicting in particular the implementation of these systems in predictive policing and medicine.

In light of this, it should become clear that to casually refer to 'AI' is to be rather vague. Willingly or not, when spelling the letters 'AI' one refers to a specific approach to simulating human cognition, implemented by means of a particular type of machine learning algorithm. In less common but more powerfully evocative cases, some people refer to 'AI' to conjure up an immaterial, more-than-human, fictional agent that plays out disparate roles in the human imagery, from forthcoming god to existential threat, from prodigal child to innovative creator. Other times, especially in the snappy conversations saturating the online space, these two definitions may mix up to various degrees, propelled by sketchy media headlines and savvy-sounding CEO's tweets. On the other hand, scientists and researchers tend to adhere to precise naming, for there exist a myriad of different machine learning and probabilistic algorithms, each with particular

---

4   More precisely, Gaussian noise is used. This is a form of signal noise where, from a statistical viewpoint, the values that noise can take are 'normally distributed'. This means that the most common values are near the mean, while less common ones are farther away from it.

affordances and limitations. Throughout this text, I will use the term *AI* to refer to deep learning algorithms or systems made out of those algorithms. When using inverted commas, as in *'AI'*, I will be referring to the popular definition of the technology as a myth. When speaking of a particular algorithm I will specify the name and type.

3. Navigating the Manifold

The emergence of corporate AI aesthetics is a result of recent research and production of particular deep learning models for natural language processing (GPT-3 by OpenAI, BERT[5] by Google), computer vision and image synthesis (Dall-e by OpenAI, Stable Diffusion by Stability AI, and Midjourney). For the sake of clarity, in this article I will focus on image generators based on probabilistic machine learning. Yet, the analysis may be useful in other case studies, for the theoretical scaffold of image-based systems is shared by other generative and predictive AI systems. In the past ten years, the perceived quality of AI-based image synthesis has increased greatly. But, possibly, what transformed a quirky way of manipulating images into a popular form of supposed 'art' is, ironically, something that has little to do with art or creativity. Recent image generators can be prompted with short text to 'generate' a matching image; and they do so by duplicating and overlapping features of existent artworks. This trick makes them appear to 'understand' semantic relations in text and to express them via images. Suddenly, an image generator model acquires a new form of alterity, moving 'AI' closer to the myth of singularity. It is less clear what art has to do with it and, hopefully, what follows can aid this line of enquiry.

In order to set up an aesthetic analysis of AI artefacts, it is important to understand how this kind of models create images. Contrary to popular opinion, a model does not create an image out of thin air; it amalgamates abstract features of existing artworks into pastiches. It is useful to recall here that image generators function according to a connectionist approach. So, rather than creating an image using logic, symbols and proto-intent as a symbolic approach would require, the generators derive images from datasets using probabilistic functions. The mechanics of this process is extremely intricate, for it depends on arbitrarily defined interactions between diverse algorithmic components. In contrast to the myth of 'AI' as a singular agent, these systems are crowded assemblages of algorithms and models that are compounded most often according to empirical experiments. Below, I describe the image generation process of a latent text-to-image

---

5   Bidirectional Encoder Representations from Transformers. It is used for Google's search engine and is widely adopted as basic tool for natural language processing research.

diffusion model, which is the most successful and widely adopted model at the time of this writing. My description, I hope, is accessible to a general reader, while staying true to the technical operations and dispensing with some details for sake of space. For the curious reader, I provide references to the implementation of the relevant algorithms. Analysing how these models work unveils a labyrinthine dramaturgy of modern computation, weaving together probability theory, visual culture and labour exploitation.

First is the data collection phase. Images of artworks and random content are scraped from the web together with the Alt-text that describe them (cf. Schuman et al. 2021). Combining images with captions into data pairs is crucial to these systems, for it is recurring captions that enable the model to track the contents of an image and thus establish links between textual semantics and visual representation. 'Daringly' challenging the established notions of authorship, images and Alt-text are collected without authors' consent. In the process, millions of artworks by living and dead artists are expropriated, in particular those working with two-dimensional imagery. To understand the scale of the scraping consider that LAION5[6], the database used by the Stable Diffusion model, includes 5.85 billion image-text pairs (LAION 2022). A subset of this database, LAION-Aesthetics, contains a collection of 600 million images[7] selected—by another machine learning model—for the reason of being 'aesthetically pleasing images' (ibid). A powerful backlash from living artists and artistic communities has unfolded through increasingly publicly actions, but, so far, it has not been 'persuasive' enough in the eyes of the models' owners.

Second, the system establishes relations between the semantic content of Alt-text and the visual content of images. Both Dall-e and Stable Diffusion perform this phase using the CLIP[8] neural network designed by OpenAI (Radford et al. 2021). Images and Alt-texts are encoded, meaning that they are described using mathematical representations. Practically, images and captions are encoded into separate numerical vectors where numbers describe some of their features; these are called 'embeddings'. What is key to my analysis here is that the model's engineers have little agency over which features the model recognizes or disregards. The model itself does not 'know' either, for it statistically manipulates probabilistic distributions in ways that are too complex to trace. "[I]t's not actually clear

---

6   The dataset can be explored using this demo https://rom1504.github.io/clip-retrieval/?back=https%3A%2F%2Fknn5.laion.ai&index=laion5B&useMclip=false&query=by+Francis+Bacon

7   According to a recent survey of a subset of the latter collection, most images are scraped from Pinterest (8.5%) and Wordpress-hosted websites (6.8%), while the rest originates from varied locations including artists-oriented platforms like DeviantArt, Flickr, Tumblr, as well as art shopping sites, including Fine Art America (5.8%), Shopify, Squarespace and Etsy.

8   Contrastive Language-Image Pre-training

what is making the AI models work well. It's not [...] clear what parts of the data are actually giving [the model] what abilities", stated David Holz, Midjourney's founder (Claburn 2022). The incomprehensibility of the model's operation increases as the process progresses. The neural network works the whole dataset so as to compute the probability that a given text embedding is the description of a given image embedding[9]. Once it completed its training, CLIP is capable of returning the most fitting caption for a given image.

The last step before generating an image is to link a user's live prompt to particular visual contents found in the dataset. Using another neural network, called Prior, a user's prompt is mapped to an image embedding and then fed to a decoder. The decoder uses the image embeddings to condition its search of visual components to sample across the dataset. Put simply, the decoder uses words to navigate the labels in the datasets and find the required image components. At the moment, the most used decoder is a diffusion model called Glide, also developed by OpenAI (Nichol et al. 2021). The diffusion process is rather convoluted, but in essence it consists of digitally manipulating visual Gaussian noise until its mathematical representation matches the text and image embeddings created by CLIP after the user's prompt. The diffusion process is perhaps better understood as filtering rather than generation. The model filters Gaussian noise iteratively so as to make it as similar as possible to selected samples of other artworks.

Thinking in a more abstract fashion can help grasp the mechanism of 'learning' and 'generation'. What happens, conceptually, is that the model groups text-image vectors by similarity or co-variance and positions the groups in a high-dimensional space. This is a virtual space called 'manifold' and can be thought of as a geometrical representation of a curvilinear and continuous space. Filling the space of the manifold is akin to constructing a cartography of the dataset, where bits of images and texts are distributed at particular locations according to particular probability densities. The manifold, therefore, contains all the image combinations that are possible with the data at hand. As a crude example, imagine the following (which I document with images in Fig. 1-2-3 below). Multiple images of a painting of a dog by Francis Bacon are grouped at one location in the manifold; multiple images of a flower by Georgia O'Keefe are grouped at another location. But a point in the manifold exists where Bacon's dogs and O'Keefe's flowers meet. When a user prompts the model to generate 'a dog by Francis Bacon in a flower by Georgia O'Keefe', the model uses the text as directions to find that particular location where dogs and flowers live next to each other. Then, it progressively samples some of the visual features stored at this location and uses them to incrementally filter Gaussian noise in the form of a matching image. The sampling is stochastic, meaning that the samples are randomly selected from the relevant data

---

9   This is done by maximizing higher probability distributions and minimizing the lower ones.

available; this is why a model prompted with the same text will always generate a different result.

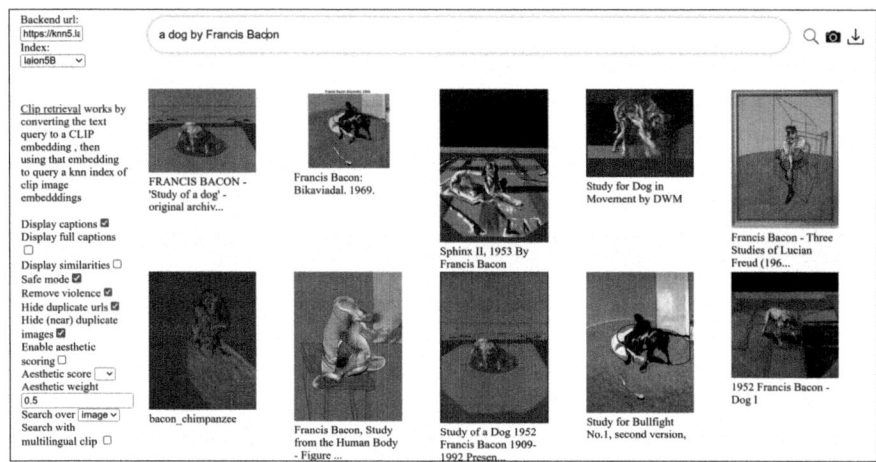

Fig. 1: *Exploring the LAION5B dataset. Top search results for 'a dog by Francis Bacon'*

Fig. 2: *Top search results for 'a flower by Georgia O'Keefe'*

Fig. 3: First four output images produced by StableDiffusion upon the prompt: 'a dog by Francis Bacon in a flower by Georgia O'Keefe'.

4. Indifference through Repetition

Unsurprisingly, given their mode of operation as described above, the image artefacts produced by AI generators exhibit sophisticated mimicry of human-made artworks or imagery. The output of these system ranges wildly in quality. Most appealing images are obtained only through numerous trials with different ways of phrasing prompts and iterating variations on initially crude outputs. Curating the output of AI generators in order to select useful images is more human-labour intensive than producing the images. Eventually, a refined AI image may show a control of composition, style and colour palettes, coupled with a polished look and delicate visual intricacies. In these cases, the models' capacity for mimicry is so uncanny that, at first, it may even suggest that the system is actually creating something new. Having demystified the mechanics behind the process, it is evident that there is no artistry at play, at least not in the way it is commonly understood in the cultures of human animals. While it is true that, in view of such a technology, the historical definition of artistry may be expanded, it is important to remain focused on the exploitation that these systems rely on; what these models perform, technically and conceptually, is a brute appropriation and a chancy exploitation of cultural capital and cultural ecosystems. Their capacity for mimesis is closer to a happy accident than to a creative stimulus or an emergent quality of software, for these algorithms are designed to recreate an amalgam of what already exists. In these AI pastiches, what may be perceived as artistic meaning is a by-product of a stochastic sampling of thousands of artists' works. The features extracted from the original artworks are drastically decontextualised, displacing, thus, the artworks' aspirations and modes of expression. Alienated remains of artistic expression are then repeated, superimposed on themselves times and times over, until they loose expressivity and become mere signs, ghostly traces of artistic intention. As signs devoid of intention, they bear an eerie detachment from human creativity. It is a process that creates, freely paraphrasing Gilles Deleuze (1968 [1994]), indifference through repetition.

In fact, such a eerie detachment from artistic intention may be one of the factors that makes AI artefacts popular. The eerie, as Mark Fisher (2016) elaborated, can be understood as a 'failure' of presence or absence. It is the feeling that something that should be there is absent, or, vice versa, something that should not be there is present. When observing an artwork, one expects, consciously or not, the artist's intention to be present in the piece. The presence of artistic intention is the *causa sine qua non* art making happens. Intention, in my view, is independent from artistry and skill levels and it emerges from one's interaction with others—living beings, materials, cultures. It can be more or less manifest and, still, be sensed in amateur artworks and less artistically successful pieces, for it is the expression of an ecosystem of relations; ultimately, artistic intention may be understood as the expression of a *collective otherness*. I will return to this in the last section when discussing two AI-based artworks whose approaches exemplify the importance of relations and otherness in art making. What is important here is that because of the way in which neural networks wrestle encoded meaning out of actual artworks, AI aesthetics rests on a mutilation of those ecosystemic creative relations that make an artwork what it is. AI aesthetics rests on a forced absence of collective otherness, for the material, cultural and personal relations that contribute to it are discarded. Where there used to be a creative goal, an artistic tradition or a rebellion against it, a chain of entangled influences (and misappropriations) across histories and cultures, nothing is left. Instead, AI image generators rely on the tired myth of the individual artist as a lonely genius. If *the* artist's intention is missing, what kind of agency created the artefact? As speculation and curious doubt are stimulated in the observers, they risk forgetting about the art itself and becoming lost in yet another old myth, that of AI singularity with its clumsy baggage exploding with anticipation over machine domination or salvation. The less romantic reality is that among the different agencies at play—computational, human, material and cultural—the one with less control over the expressivity of AI aesthetics is the computational. For it is the AI complex, with its human, material and cultural agencies, its networks and interests that conceives, designs and fosters how current AI image generation works, how it is disseminated, understood and exploited. The algorithmic system itself functions as a combinatorial agent, enmeshing features of artistic expression with the desires, beliefs and investments of the AI complex. Paradoxically, the algorithmic system does embody an ecosystem of relations, that of the AI complex. This, admittedly, has not much to do with creativity.

The absence of a creative vision in AI artefacts, as well as the presence of normative power in the AI complex, can also be observed in the way AI generative systems cautiously mimic traditional and trending aesthetic criteria[10]. What they offer is *little enough* variation to tickle curiosity, but never enough to unsettle standards. The automated process of mimesis performed by AI generators conflates aesthetic languages, vocabularies, forms and structures of disparate artworks into a single form, while leaving them unchanged and unchallenged at the same time. What this operation offers, artistically and aesthetically, is the safety of what one already knows, combined with the thrill of a more or less riskless adventure. It recalls trophy hunting, where entitled individuals can experience the thrill of killing magnificent animals in the wild through the safety glass of a four-wheel drive. In this sense, AI aesthetics exists comfortably within the reign of what Ursula Le Guin (2001: XV) once described as "commodified fantasy", a form of cultural production that

takes no risks: it invents nothing, but imitates and trivializes. It proceeds by depriving the old stories of their intellectual and ethical complexity, turning their truth-telling to sentimental platitude. [...] Profoundly disturbing moral choices are sanitized, made cute, made safe.

The supposed novelty heralded by AI image generators is a kind of change that ends in and with itself; it is sanitized, safe and claustrophobically self-referential. In reproducing ad infinitum the stuff of existent artworks recombined in infinitely slight variations, AI generators make reference only to their own capacity to do so. Following Deleuze (1981: 33) in his analysis of Bacon's paintings, one can see that the self-referentiality of AI generators is alien to *sensations:* those granules of expression or sensory particles traced across an artwork by the embodied act of making, effectively a form of corporeal expression that AI generators expunge from the source artworks they use. It is sensations that guide an observer's perception of the rhythms and intensities expressed by a particular artwork. These, in turn, help reveal how the artwork's concepts, symbols, desires or ways of dealing with them configure themselves into a dynamics of relation—engaging distant living beings, cultures and ideas (Donnarumma 2020). Being void of sensation, AI generators fall short of the aesthetic and sensorial force of art to bring about a questioning or a consequence. A close look at most AI artefacts, in fact, shows them to be neither drastically new forms of digital painting, illustration or generative art nor manifestly innovative ways of conceiving visual representation. These

---

10 The idiom "trending on ArtStation" is one of the most used parts of textual prompts by users of Midjourney.

artefacts do not require the creation of a new vocabulary to be described; on the contrary, they can only be characterised by means of well-known, pre-existent tropes and references. Their awe-inducing familiarity and their unchallenging mode of expression is what makes them so conceptually appealing and financially attractive to the AI complex. I expand on this point below, when discussing the art market.

As far as the vexed question goes: is AI capable of making art? I side with Joanna Zylinska (2020: 49) to state that this is a "misguided question". As I wrote in the introduction to this article, these kinds of questions distract from deeper issues about the AI complex and the way it operates through and onto culture. That said, I think it is helpful to analyse how and where the question of creativity arises, for it may help reveal another principle of corporate AI aesthetics. So, who poses those misguided questions and how do they benefit from it? The deep learning science community is generally weary of mystification. While it could greatly benefit from further developing its working definitions of art, labour and culture, and this impetus is growing within the discipline, a cursory reading of the technical papers referred to earlier quickly shows that researchers are above all interested in models' functionality, operation and optimization. It is rare to see AI scientists making claims of superhuman intelligence or human-like creativity. As expected, these kinds of claims are more often tied to the hype cycles across the industry PR and the mass media landscape. Less expected is to find, as sometimes happens, such claims among artists, curators and producers in media art. For, arguably, this artistic practice was born out of a paradigm that challenged the consumer-ready myth of endless technological progress sold by large part of the industry.

Tellingly, the trope of human-like creativity or singularity-level intelligence is most often found among those working directly or in close contact with the art market, an important agent within the AI complex. The most recent sale operation by auction house Sotheby's involves "the world's first intelligent NFT [...] coded with its own personality", "a modern day Alice [in Wonderland]" that ushers in "the age of living, self-learning artwork" (Sotheby's 2022). Or so we are told. Another sale operation by Sotheby's describes an AI generated video work as using an "AI brain" which is a "self-contained creative agent" enthusing collectors by offering them "the opportunity to watch an AI brain 'think' in real time" (Sothebys 2018). Leaving aside the courageous copy-editing, this precisely crafted language suggests something intriguing about what actually may be the focus of attention. It signals that perhaps when it comes to art as a commodity and source of financial capital, corporate AI aesthetics has indeed a unique value: the allure of a human-made machine that can "think". Tragic as it is, in this context, deceit and speculation are the real commodities, while art remain a marginally relevant, haunted shell. But there is another almost antithetical side to the art market exploitation of the AI race. On occasion of the first sale of an AI-generated artwork at the auction house Christies, the organiser of the sale, Richard Lloyd, was asked whether the art market saw a future for AI-generated images. He replied, 'It may not have been painted by a man in a powdered wig, but it is exactly the kind of artwork we have been selling for 250 years' (Christies 2018). It is strikingly ironic, albeit unsurprising, that a supposed ground-breaking artwork owns its fame and price to the fact that it replicates the most conventional kind of painting in the art market. Sameness pays.

As a form of expression of the power and capital dynamics of the AI complex, corporate AI aesthetics has quickly come to dominate the cultural and artistic landscape. This is the most seriously troubling aspect to it. If AI generators were only marketed as plug-ins, as tools that excel at a particular kind of image manipulation, critical appraisal may not be needed. The technology would even perhaps become an empowering tool, for it can certainly provide a gentle and playful entry point to algorithmic art. The problem, more important than the one concerning what this specific technology does, is who owns it or funds it and who produces it. AI generators are, at the time of this writing, a monopoly of a few extremely wealthy corporations or individuals who can afford the resources to pay for research, computational power, legal protection, viral marketing and appealing testimonials. The aesthetics these tools express quickly becomes, therefore, culturally dominant; in other words, it becomes the norm.

5. Normalizing the Future by refracting the Past

[A]lgorithms act, but they do so as part of an ill-defined network of actions upon actions, part of a complex of power-knowledge relations, in which unintended consequences, like the side effects of a program's behavior, can become critically important. (Goffey 2008: 19)

Because AI systems are human-made constructs that can create consequences in the world, they are always active agents. Rather than being neutral tools or independent agents decontextualised from social life, they are imbued with a precise and pluripotent agency. This draws from the particular world views of the people—and their arrangements, such disciplines of study, epistemes or capitalist abstractions - who fund, design, program and implement them. In today's capitalistic societies, deep and probabilistic learning systems are a material substrate (as in surveillance infrastructures, server farms, data networks) and an organizational scaffold (as in the structuring of policies, business plans, trends and trade strategies). Therefore, the agency of those systems helps materialise the very same worldviews that originated them. In other words, predictive systems construct the world by acting in it. Chun (2021) elaborates at length, for example, on how predictive policing systems act in the intimate lives of people by creating polarization and augmenting the vulnerability of those already vulnerable. Similarly, I argue, image generators act within the cultural texture of societies by reinforcing biases in visual culture, abstracting artistic labour and chipping at the idea of creativity as a collective, intergenerational and trans-cultural process until nothing remains of it.

It is not a coincidence that the advent of deep and probabilistic learning in artistic communities is taking place at a time when nuances have become the poorest currency in the cultural arena. Arguably, this may partly be the result of the widespread use of probabilistic and deep learning models across structural components of capitalistic societies; a feedback of sorts. The probabilistic ideology behind the architecture of AI art generators is, in fact, the same that powers predictive policing systems (ibid: 153), surveillance systems by Palantir (Iliadis/ Acker, 2022), parts of the financial market, social media timelines from Tik Tok to Facebook and film and music recommendation systems such as Spotify and Netflix. By means of these platforms, social and cultural life becomes largely and silently influenced, and sometimes even driven, by machinic predictions based on past information. The effect is a tight enclosing of social and cultural groups and their isolation from one another according to data from their past activities, clicks and likes. More than just a way of doing computation, it seems that the probabilistic learning view is turning into an invisible dogma. It pervades and regulates societies at a political, social and cultural level.

What is the potential of this societal shift and which role does AI aesthetics play in it? A perspective I want to suggest, especially in view of the recent dissemination of highly disruptive chatbot generators such as ChatGPT, Bing and Bard, is that AI aesthetics functions as soft propaganda. It would make sense, from the viewpoint of the AI complex, to stir public opinion, to domesticate it by means of a playful version of an AI probabilistic system, before raising the stakes with untested, unstable and 'hallucinating' language systems. It is such an uncanny coincidence that image generators inundated the cultural, media and social discourse just a little in advance of the massively public launch of large language models, which had been in development since several years. What is certain is that corporate AI aesthetics has been mediatically and culturally transfigured into a proxy for human-like creativity. While criticism of these systems is widespread, the work of large AI models is now commonly understood as a friendly, familiar, innocuous and innovative way of opening up creativity. At closer inspection, however, it is clear that the aesthetics of probabilistic systems is a closure for creativity rather than an opening. It can be understood as an operational schemata that is parasitic of cultural output: it uses repetition and imitation to bring about an aesthetic and conceptual normalization of a new that is a cheap duplicate of the present - and past. Echoing Fisher (2009) once more: this copy-paste of the present onto itself repeated infinite times brings about a forgetfulness of the injustices of the past and a foreclosure of the possibilities of the future. It normalizes a future of sameness by refracting the sanitized past ad nauseam.

For critical disability scholar Margrit Shildrick (2002: 71), "we are all implicated on an everyday level in a process of discursive othering that serves to establish and perpetuate standards of normativity". Discursive othering can be understood as a multilayered form of discrimination against those 'other' than the productive white Western able male: BIPOC, elderly, disabled (by society), queer and non-binary, poor, lower class people. This kind of discrimination is discursive because it propagates the enforcement of normativity through words, images, patterns and systems that are *implicitly* discriminatory. The historical connection between eugenics, statistics and AI is an excellent illustration of how ideological racism can turn into discursive othering. This is a widely known history, surprisingly simple to trace yet little talked about. Theoretical and mathematical concepts elaborated by prominent eugenists, including two founders of eugenics, Francis Galton and Karl Pearson, provided the scaffold for modern statistics (MacKenzie 1981; Davis 1995: 30; Chun 2021: 59). These concepts include notions such as linear regression, correlation and principal component analysis[11] found today at the core of deep learning techniques that, as mentioned earlier, are heavily dependent on statistical methods.

Incidentally, the nemesis of data regression and discrimination—the latter is the technical term for classification—is something named 'outlier', a piece of data that does not fit the norm and therefore corrupts statistical reasoning. The outlier stays in the way of statistical truth, whereas the ideal lies in an average of probabilities. The more a piece of data or a person deviates from a norm the more they enter the domain of deviancy, of the extreme. Those people, thing or data, which can only exist at the edges surrounding the average become, thus, synonymous with the untrue, irrelevant, something that can be safely discarded. Following this logic, deep learning algorithms used for data classification must have layers that "amplify aspects of the input that are important for discrimination and suppress *irrelevant variations*" (Lecun et al. 2015: 436 [emphasis added]). Which are the criteria according to which a variation is deemed irrelevant? Far from being a semantic problem, the key question is, who has the power to establish relevance and irrelevance, to define the norm?

These questions become more poignant when considered in conjunction with the fact that, historically, the development of foundational AI theories and infrastructural AI technologies has been largely at the hand of Western, white males (Katz 2020)—with the exception of robotics, a field that owes much to diverse research communities, in particular those in Japan. Today, researchers in the field come from more varied background and geographical locations and yet, a techno-deterministic and reductionist mentality seems to remain dominant. As a result, parts of that field apply and amplify rooted biases and more or less latent forms of discrimination that, with or without malicious intent, have plagued deep learning since its re-emergence—although have not perturbed its pervasiveness.

---

11   Other concepts include standard deviation, p-values, chi-squared mean, and more exists.

This reflection is not meant to claim the existence of a suppressed or militant racism at the core of probabilistic theory or deep learning. Many researchers in those field are well intentioned if not actively striving to counter forms of computational othering (Bender et al. 2021) or the ambiguous creative power of Big Data (Vigliensoni et al. 2022) and their work must be supported and disseminated. More subtly, my observation is meant to focus attention on how deep learning, following statistics with its roots in eugenics, creates and disseminates a world view where people, images, sounds, money, lives - anything that is and is made countable - can be precisely understood and predicted. What is required is 'only' a large amount of data and related computational capacity coupled with a clear assumption of what a usefully functioning, a newly normative pattern will look like. This new kind of norm still often is, or refers to, what Wynter (2015: 19) aptly defines as a "single genre-specific Western [...] bourgeois model of being", or, in other words, a capitalist, conformed, productive and consumer individual; a blueprint that is not only adopted in the West, Global North and most capitalist societies but also imposed on the others.

It is only from a perspective wherein anything can be algorithmically predicted because it is ascribed to only one particular mode of being—that of the capitalist, conformed and productive worldview—that it may become reasonable to think that an AI system with access to billions of images and artworks, but entirely lacking in intention, ideas, a sense of self and, most importantly, embodied relations to others, can attain creativity. Further, only within that episteme and a form of capitalism that upholds enormous concentration of power in the hands of the few, it may become acceptable to collect thousands of artworks without consent in order to train an AI system. Despite strong backlash from individual artists, whole communities and large companies,[12] the very fact of exploitation and the disregard for consent slips within the creaks of 'innovation', becoming a passing thought that can only be detrimental to this quest of control. Yet, while an ideology of prediction may help research protein folding or climate modelling, culture and art making require no ideology, but interpersonal and interspecies relations, artistic urge, socio-cultural context, outliers and outsiders, unreachable edges and indescribable thoughts.

What I find important to stress, then, is that AI aesthetics functions as an effective means of enforcement of knowledge, in particular of the system of

---

12 Well known illustration artists Simon Stalenhag and RJ Palmer have been publicly vocal about the exploitation issue, while administrators of the online artistic communities Fur Affinity and Newgrounds rewrote their policies to explicitly ban "AI art". Two among the most popular communities, DeviantArt and ArtStation are facing increasing pressure from their users to enact a similar ban. More recently Getty Images has sued StabilityAI for unlawfully copying and processing millions of their copyrighted images.

knowledge that defines neoliberal societies; an order based on the repetition and normalization of the Western understanding of cognitive and aesthetic criteria. It is telling in this sense that the parameters of scientific evaluation of the generative capability of the popular diffusion models are limited to the degree of realism or photorealism, samples diversity and similarity to users' caption (Ramesh et al. 2021, 2022). When considered scientifically, aesthetic quality evaluation is automated (ibid: 13) and when it is not, it is based on individual, unmotivated assumptions of what beauty is or should be; as Holz illustrates "I do think the world needs more beauty. Basically, if I create something that allows people to make beautiful things, and there are more beautiful things in the world, that's what I want *by default*." (Claburn 2022 [emphasis added]). What Holz speaks about is a vision of a stale, normalised beauty that can and *should be* universalised through technology. What is missing from the picture is that beauty is far from universal and that, depending on who is looking, the world may already be full of it, while in the process of actively destroying it. With each new seeming or actual breakthrough rippling through media outlets, the AI complex normalises a universalist view of human cognition, machinic agency and aesthetic values, involving scientists, artists and workers across generations in the process. It provides scientific proof for a reductionist understanding of cognition and embodiment, all the way to notions of intelligence, beauty and creativity. To validate itself, the AI complex outputs scientific research and artistic artefacts with little space for counterarguments or criticism; as shown by the routine of frantically publishing research lacking peer review and hyperbolic descriptions of artworks.

Fig. 4: First output image produced by Dall-e with the prompt: 'capitalism reflected in an infinity mirror'

AI aesthetics, encroached as it is between techno-determinism and capital, has users, viewers and customers implicated in the perpetuation of the illusion of exponential progress, a view oblivious to the significant contribution of the AI complex to societal polarization, undermining of human and workers' rights and the current climate collapse. By equating sophisticated mimicry to a neoliberal reductionist conception of creativity, the AI complex exploits art as yet another distraction from the dramatic and largely irreversible impact of its technologies on humans and non-humans. Here AI aesthetics functions as an epistemic infinity mirror (Fig. 4). It creates receding reflections of the technocratic order of knowledge, amplifying it to infinity within a small, rigid and inescapable frame.

6. Against the Norm

Machines, the entire technology of the West, is just that, the technology of the West. Nothing *has* to look or function the way it does. The West man's freedom, unscientifically got at the expense of the rest of the world's people, has allowed him to expand his mind— spread his sensibility wherever it go, & so *shaped* the world, & its powerful artifact-engines. (Baraka 1970)

Deep learning, and artificial intelligence at large, do not have to be conceived and designed in the way they are. As elaborated throughout this text and as Baraka's powerful and prescient statement above reinforces, the present embodiment of deep learning and its expressive capacities are defined by specific powers. These, that I gather under the term AI complex, are the powers owning the financial, cultural and political means of computational production, and therefore those set out to gain unhinged profits from it. What art practice needs to counter this narrative, in addition to awareness and literacy, is the willingness to imagine a radically different present and therefore an alternative future. As illuminated by Fisher (2009), capitalism does not limit itself to the regulation of politics and finance. Rather, it is a pervasive atmosphere, a material and immaterial ambiance that severs imagination from culture, work and education; what Fisher calls "capitalist realism". As a strategy to ensure its own resilience, the doctrine of capitalist realism has erected a "grey curtain" (ibid: 81) over the horizon of possible futures that exists beyond capitalism itself. What is needed in media art and elsewhere, therefore, is rigorous work on imagining alternative ways to perverse the current route of AI technologies. Through this kind of imagination untamed ways of thinking about the meaning of technologically mediated art in times of environmental disruption will emerge. These ways will have little to do with the established canons of Western beauty or unfounded clamours of human-like machine intelligence. These are ways that will call into action the creative work of collectivities, the intelligent non-human entities that live in the world, and the limitations and potentials of deep learning to envision and manipulate polyphonic futures.

As brief case studies, in closing this article I want to discuss two artworks, *In Search of Good Ancestors / Ahnen in Arbeit* by Jonathan Chaim Reus (2022) and *Aerodinámicas de las Semilla* by the artist group Electrobiota (2023). Through their imagination, these works are capable of creating new, collective knowledge that can sculpt realities.

Reus is a transmedia artist and musician, originally from the US and based in the Netherlands. His piece *In Search of Good Ancestors* works technically and socially with the idea of machine learning algorithms as unstable memory. It enquires into the intergenerational implications of voice datasets and it does so by inviting interested strangers to literally seed and participate in the evolution of the work. The work consists of a 24-hour radio stream of generative speech broadcast over a year.[13] The voice that can be heard on the stream is generated using deep learning models for text and speech. Initially, the models generated new vocal content starting from a lecture by US virologist Jonas Salk, where he calls for Western cultures to emphasise intergenerational responsibility as a high moral imperative. Rather than mulling over endless variations of the original text, throughout the ensuing year the model is gradually fed new, small voice and text datasets that Reus creates from scratch together with the participants of his public workshops. As its dataset is replaced time after time, the model is fine-tuned to continuously update its predictions. Machine memory becomes unstable, collective and collectivised. Because the artwork's way of rethinking deep learning technology subverts the strict paradigm of AI image generation discussed so far, *In Search of Good Ancestors* speaks about strategies whereby deep learning becomes a conceptual territory to navigate and shape, rather than a tool to be adopted as is. The workshop participants are neither deep learning nor voice experts, yet together with Reus they familiarise with the technical basis of the means and, importantly, appropriate the technology by developing personal modes of interaction with it. Together, they curate the texts for the model's training, design annotations for expressive text generation, perform with voice clones and record voice data individually and collectively (Fig. 5). As Reus explains, this format enables the diversity of languages and predisposition of the participants to enrich the process by allowing a "plurality of intentions and (literal) voices" to *become* the work (Reus 2022: 1).

Electrobiota is a transdisciplinary group of artists and researchers including Gabriela Munguía, Mario Guzmán, Guadalupe Chávez, Ángel Salazar and Erika Torres, whose bases lie across Argentina, Mexico, Ecuador and Colombia. Their work *Aerodinámicas de las Semilla* (literally translated as aerodynamics of seeds) is a multifaceted project aiming to generate alternative perspectives on intelligence by looking carefully at plants and their reproduction processes and technologies. The work output takes multiple. interrelated forms: a generative website, a database

---

13 The work can be experienced at https://ahnen.in/

of real and speculative flying seeds specimen, and an accompanying collection of texts that recombine, through deep learning, existing manuscripts on botanics, ecology, philosophy and poetry.[14] Rather than leveraging AI generators to create the kind of beauty that Holz dreamed of, Electrobiota deploys that technology to create speculative morphologies of some of the flying seeds native to their lands, as well as to catalogue and describe them. Every time a user visits the website, the model changes the textual descriptions by recombining them in always novel configurations. In doing so, Electrobiota purposely plays with the core of scientific explanation and visualisation, and, by implication, of scientific knowledge.

Fig. 5: *The artist and the participants at one of Reus' project workshop sessions as they prepare to record voice material.*

Similarly to Reus' work, Electrobiota's interest lies not in the technology per se, but in a collaborative action that generates a form of collective otherness. In this case, it is about an exploration of the territories that the plants inhabit and the artists share with them. Together with biologists and biodiversity researchers, they set out to collect specimen of indigenous flying seeds across their own native lands (Fig. 6).

Their travel through those territories soon morphed into a new reading of the land that followed, conceptually and physically, the relations among the non-human lives inhabiting it; a remapping of the land according to plant intelligence rather than human geopolitics. Through deep learning, the group analysed and compared the various seeds morphologies and found possible kinship relations among them. This enabled speculation on the potential for resilience and dissemination of some morphological features, providing an insight into possible ways in which the plants may evolve their reproductive organs; an urgent topic given the extreme

---

14 The work lives at https://aerodynamics-of-seeds.netlify.app/

violence to biodiversity provoked by the global environmental changes. The aesthetic and poetic power of the work rests, therefore, on its methodology: as the group puts it (Electrobiota 2023), they use artificial intelligence to "negotiate otherness". The focus is not on the capability of the machine per se, but on its affordances in aiding the exploration, understanding and negotiation of plant intelligence. Simply put, the machine is a means to facilitate an intimate view into the existence of non-human others, fostering, in the process, strategies of curiosity, care and imagination.

Fig. 6: Electrobiota photographing seeds of Tipa in order to catalogue them and feed them to a deep learning system to generate further, speculative specimen. Courtesy of the artists.

Both works, *In Search of Good Ancestors* and *Aerodinámicas de las Semilla*, speak effectively against the norm of corporate AI aesthetics. They do so in different ways and yet share roots in a fundamental embodiedness of the artistic experience. Being in the world as a relational and attentive entity among many others is posited as the spark of audacious relationships: between workshop participants, voices and AI models or between text and memories in the case of Reus' work, and among artists and biologists and land or among seeds and algorithms in the case of Electrobiota. This is an aesthetic of relationality (Donnarumma 2020: 41), for it embraces the affordances of deep learning from a viewpoint of profound awareness of one's embodiment and interdependence in the world. Thus, rather than masking or mystifying the mechanisms of algorithmic agency, this kind of aesthetics utilizes, excavates and subverts that agency for what it is: codified instructions for patterns matching in a world of living things. This strategy does not trivialise the capacity of deep learning. On the contrary, and perhaps counter-intuitively, by laying naked the bare bones of deep learning systems and making them vulnerable and attuned to other kinds of agencies - human, vegetal and material - algorithmic agency is made an integral part of a new sensory clutch. It becomes a means of grasping the limits of memory, the multiplicities of identity, the intelligence of a plant or the histories of a flying seed (Fig. 7).

Fig. 7: *Microscope photography of a seed of a Diente de león. Courtesy of Electrobiota*

Acknowledgements

This article is the result of hours of conversation with colleagues, who, with their varied expertise, constructive criticism and generous thinking supported my research. I thank the Intelligent Instruments Lab for allowing me the time to work on this manuscript during my residency there, and in particular Victor Shepardson, Jack Armitage and Thor Magnusson for our exchanges. I am grateful to Olga Goriunova for our conversations and her insightful reading of this manuscript. A warm thanks goes also to Minerva H. Trejo, Elizabeth Jochum and Pablo Gobira for their suggestions, Jonathan Chaim Reus and Electrobiota for their time and thoughts, and the journal's reviewers for their feedback.

References

Baraka, A. (1970): "Technology & Ethos." Vol. 2 Book of Life. In: Raise Rage Rays Raze: Essays Since 1965.

Bender, E. M., Gebru, T., McMillan-Major, A., and Shmitchell, S. (2021): "On the dangers of stochastic parrots: Can language models be too big?" In: FAccT 2021 - Proceedings of the 2021 ACM Conference on Fairness, Accountability, and Transparency, 1, pp. 610-623.

Blyth, S. (2018): "Big Data and Machine Learning Won't Save Us from Another Financial Crisis." Harvard Business School Cases. (https://hbr.org/2018/09/big-data-and-machine-learning-wont-save-us-from-another-financial-crisis)

Cambridge Analytica (2022). "Leave.EU: Psychographic Targeting for Britain." (https://www.parliament.uk/globalassets/documents/commons-committees/culture-media-and-sport/BK-Background-paper-CA-proposals-to-LeaveEU.pdf).

Caramiaux, B./Donnarumma, M. (2021): "Artificial Intelligence in Music and Performance: A Subjective Art-Research Inquiry". In: E. R. Miranda (ed.), Handbook of Artificial Intelligence for Music. Foundations, Advanced Approaches, and Developments for Creativity. London: Springer, pp. 75-95.

Casilli, A. A./Posada Gutiérrez, J. (2019): "The Platformization Of Labor and Society." In: Graham, Mark & Dutton, William H. (eds.), Society and the Internet: How Networks of Information and Communication are Changing Our Lives, (2nd edition). Oxford: Oxford University Press, pp. 293-306.

Christie's (2018): "Is artificial intelligence set to become art's next medium?" (https://www.christies.com/features/a-collaboration-between-two-artists-one-human-one-a-machine-9332-1.aspx).

Chun, W. H. K. (2021): Discriminating Data: Correlation, neighborhoods, and the new politics of recognition. Cambridge: MIT Press.

Claburn, T. (2022): "David Holz, founder of AI art generator Midjourney, on the future of imaging." The Register. (https://www.theregister.com/2022/08/01/david_holz_midjourney/).

Davis, L. J. (1995): Enforcing Normalcy: Disability, Deafness, and the Body. London: Verso.

Deleuze, G. (1968): *Différence et répétition*. Paris: PUF. Tr. as *Difference and Repetition*, by Paul Patton (1994). New York: Columbia University Press.

Deleuze, G. (1981): Francis Bacon: The Logic of Sensation. Paris: Editions de la Difference.

Donnarumma, M. (2020): "Across Bodily and Disciplinary Borders: Hybridity as methodology, expression, dynamic". Performance Research 25/4, pp. 36-44.

Fisher, M. (2009): Capitalist Realism. London: Repeater Books.

Fisher, M. (2016): The Weird and the Eerie. London: Zero Books.

Goffey, A. (2008): "Algorithm". In: M. Fuller (ed.), Software Studies - A Lexicon. Cambridge: MIT Press.

Hoijtink, M./Planqué-Van Hardeveld, A. (2022): "Machine Learning and the Platformization of the Military: A Study of Google's Machine Learning Platform TensorFlow." International Political Sociology 16/2, pp. 1-19.

Hu, M. (2020): "Cambridge Analytica's black box." Big Data and Society 7/2, pp. 1-6.

Iliadis, A./Acker, A. (2022): "The seer and the seen: Surveying Palantir's surveillance platform." The Information Society, pp. 1-30.

Kai Y. (2013): "Large-scale deep learning at Baidu." In: Proceedings of the 22nd ACM international conference on Information & Knowledge Management (CIKM '13). New York: Association for Computing Machinery, pp. 2211-2212.

Katz, Y. (2020): Artificial Whiteness: Politics and Ideology in Artificial Intelligence. New York: Columbia University Press.

Le Guin, U. K. (2021): Earthsea: Tales from Earthsea. Cycle #5. New York: Graphia.

Lecun, Y., Bengio, Y. and Hinton, G. (2015): "Deep learning". Nature 521/7553, pp. 436-444.

Lewis, J. E., Arista, N., Pechawis, A., and Kite, S. (2018): "Making Kin with the Machines". Journal of Design and Science, pp. 1-13.

Lozano-Hemmer, R. (1996): "Perverting Technological Correctness." Leonardo 29/1 pp. 5-15.

Luitse, D. and Denkena, W. (2021): "The great transformer: Examining the role of large language models in the political economy of AI." Big Data and Society 8/2, pp.1-14.

MacKenzie, D. A. (1981): Statistics in Britain, 1865-1930. Edinburgh: Edinburgh University Press.

McCarthy, J., Minsky, M. L., Rochester, N., and Shannon, C. E. (1955): "A proposal for the Dartmouth summer research project on artificial intelligence." White paper.

Milmo, D. (2022): "Social media firms 'monetising misery', says Molly Russell's father after inquest". The Guardian. (https://www.theguardian.com/uk-news/2022/sep/30/molly-russell-died-while-suffering-negative-effects-of-online-content-rules-coroner).

Nichol, A., Dhariwal, P., Ramesh, A., Shyam, P., Mishkin, P., McGrew, B., Sutskever, I., and Chen, M. (2021): "GLIDE: Towards Photorealistic Image Generation and Editing with Text-Guided Diffusion Models." White paper.

Olorunnimbe, K./Viktor, H. (2022): "Deep learning in the stock market—a systematic survey of practice, backtesting, and applications." Artificial Intelligence Review, 56, pp. 2057-2109.

Radford, A., Kim, J. W., Hallacy, C., Ramesh, A., Goh, G., Agarwal, S., Sastry, G., Askell, A., Mishkin, P., Clark, J., Krueger, G., and Sutskever, I. (2021): "Learning Transferable Visual Models From Natural Language Supervision." White paper.

Ramesh, A., Dhariwal, P., Nichol, A., Chu, C., and Chen, M. (2022): "Hierarchical Text-Conditional Image Generation with CLIP Latents." White paper.

Reus, J. C. (2022): "In Search of Good Ancestors / Ahnen in Arbeit". In: Nordic Human-Computer Interaction Conference (NordiCHI '22), October 8–12, 2022, Aarhus, Denmark. New York: ACM.

Schuhmann, C., Vencu, R., Beaumont, R., Kaczmarczyk, R., Mullis, C., Katta, A., Coombes, T., Jitsev, J., and Komatsuzaki, A. (2021): "LAION-400M: Open Dataset of CLIP-Filtered 400 Million Image-Text Pairs." White paper.

Shildrick, M. (2002): Embodying the Monster: Encounters with the Vulnerable Self. London: Sage Publications.

Smolensky, P. (1987): "Connectionist AI, symbolic AI, and the brain." Artificial Intelligence Review 1/2, pp. 95-109.

Sotheby's (2018): "Contemporary Art Day Auction / Lot 109." (https://www.sothebys.com/en/auctions/ecatalogue/2019/contemporary-art-day-auction-l19021/lot.109.html?locale=en).

Sotheby's (2022): "Meet the world's first intelligent NFT. The age of living, self-learning artwork has arrived." (https://thefirstinft.com/).

Sornette, D., and Von der Becke, S. (2011): "Computer trading: crashes and high frequency trading." UK Government Office for Science, 1-26. (https://www.gov.uk/government/publications/computer-trading-crashes-and-high-frequency-trading).

Sudmann, A. (2018): "On the Media-political Dimension of Artificial Intelligence." Digital Culture & Society, 4(1), pp. 181-200.

Vigliensoni, G., Perry, P., and Fiebrink, R. (2022): "A Small-Data Mindset for Generative AI Creative Work." Generative AI and HCI - CHI 2022 Workshop, May 10, 2022, Online 1/1, pp. 1-5.

Whittaker, M. (2021): "From ethics to organizing: getting serious about AI." Distinguished Speaker Series, Hariri Institute for Computing, Boston University, Boston, MA, United States. (https://www.youtube.com/watch?v=_BzUobDoIcs).

Wynter, S. (2015): "Yours in the Intellectual Struggle: Sylvia Wynter and the Realization of the Living." In: K. McKittrick (ed.), On Being Human As Praxis. Durham and London: Duke University Press.

Yearwood, E. L. (2022): "A whistleblower confronts social media". Archives of Psychiatric Nursing, 37(PA1).

Zou, Y., Jin, X., Li, Y., Guo, Z., Wang, E. and Xiao, B. (2014): "Mariana: tencent deep learning platform and its applications". In: Proceedings of the VLDB Endowment, 7/13, pp. 1772-1777.

Zylinska, J. (2020): AI Art. Machine Visions and Warped Dreams. London: Open Humanities Press.

The Dancer in the Machine

Simon Biggs, Sue Hawksley and Mark D. McDonnell

Abstract

This article explores questions of distributed agency in human and nonhuman assemblages. The interactive artwork 'Double Agent', by Simon Biggs, serves as both a laboratory for this exploration and as an exemplar for the discussion. Following a short introduction about 'Double Agent', and the proposition alluded to in the title of this article, the text explores concepts of creativity, agency and ontology, with particular reference to N. Katherine Hayles' proposition of cognitive assemblage and James Leach's theory of creativity. A review of recent creative projects that explore the application of machine-learning to human movement and/or incorporate embodied human machine interaction provides a background for a more detailed description of the 'Double Agent' project and a discussion of the questions and ideas that motivated its conception and arose through its development and subsequent exhibition.

Keywords

interactive art, machine-learning, dance, agency, technogenesis, distributed cognition

Introduction

Developments in autonomous technologies are leading to agency being progressively distributed from humans to machines—socially, physically and psychologically. In this context questions arise concerning how humans and machines communicate and interact with one another, and how they may engage in mutual co-creation through co-performance.

In this paper we explore these issues through a discussion centred around *Double Agent* (Biggs 2018), an interactive installation artwork by artist Simon Biggs, which employs augmented reality, interactive technologies and machine-learning systems that enable embodied human machine interaction in three-dimensional space. Novel machine-learning algorithms, when trained with suitable representations of human movement, allow elements of the system to improvise movement in response to the live actions of human interactors, including expert movers such as dancers, and to participate in an improvised dialogue as a co-creative agent.

Through development of novel machine-learning capabilities within an interactive augmented environment, the *Double Agent* project seeks to integrate the methodologies of improvisational creative arts performance and generative machine-learning to explore how distributed forms of agency and creativity, involving both human and nonhuman actors, emerge within this context.

Fig. 1: *Double Agent*, 2018, Simon Biggs, interactive installation, MOCO'19, Tempe, Arizona, USA. Performer Ziqian Zhou. (image: Simon Biggs)

Ghosts, zombies and cyborgs

The title of this paper, *The dancer in the machine*, is a play on Gilbert Ryle's phrase "the dogma of the ghost in the machine" (Ryle 2009: 5), referring to his classic critique of Cartesian dualism. Ryle argued against what he called the 'official doctrine', deriving primarily from the Cartesian 'myth' of a mind and body relationship that posits mind as a ghost within, or puppeteer of, the physical body. Ryle observed that according to the doctrine,

bodies are in space and are subject to the mechanical laws which govern all other bodies in space. Bodily processes and states can be inspected by external observers. So a man's bodily life is as much a public affair [...] But minds are not in space, nor are their operations subject to mechanical laws. The workings of one mind are not witnessable by other observers; its career is private. (ibid: 1-2)

Ryle objects that "[i]t is assumed that there are two different kinds of existence or status. What exists or happens may have the status of physical existence, or it may have the status of mental existence [...] There is thus a polar opposition between mind and matter." (ibid: 3).

Ryle's behaviourist arguments against dualism foreshadow later developments in the philosophy of mind and cognitive science, where agency is considered to be enacted not from a central, private control system (a puppeteer, or a ghost in a machine) but rather, as distributed across the subject, the social, the environment and the technological. Theorists such as Andy Clark, David Chalmers and N. Katherine Hayles, exploring concepts of cognition as dynamical, embodied, extended, distributed and situated, raise questions about automated information processing and machine-learning in relation to human and nonhuman agency. Ryle noted, in an uncanny inverse premonition of the Turing test, that following the logic of the dualist doctrine, a person could not, with the possible exception of themselves, "tell the difference between a man and a Robot" (2009: 10). This philosophical conundrum could equally apply to zombies; David Chalmers has argued that a philosophical zombie (p-zombie), as a non-sentient agent which is indistinguishable from a sentient subject, is evidence that consciousness exists beyond the physical and behavioural. His p-zombies are physical beings, and are "probably not naturally possible: they probably cannot exist in our world, with its laws of nature" (Chalmers 1996). However, with the advent of machine-learning systems possessing properties similar to those of Chalmers p-zombie, new questions arise about the potential for virtual zombies—what we might term v-zombies. In the case of the *Double Agent* project a machine creates a 'dancer' out of data, and we experience its ghostly presence through the effect it has in the interactive virtual environment that we (as the interactor) cohabit. Are we witness to the career of a disembodied machine-made mind (a 'ghost in the machine'), or is the installation haunted by a v-zombie?

N. Katherine Hayles has argued that humans and machines are coevolving as symbiotic entities, what she has termed *technogenesis*, and that subsequently cognition occurs not only within the human subject but beyond it, in its extended material, cultural and technological environment, including in linguistic and computational systems (Hayles 2012). Hayles' argument is predicated on a view of the world as an assemblage of assemblages, where things exist as contingent upon, and interwoven with, one another. This is in contrast to a view that apprehends the universe as composed of distinct bounded entities defined by their differences rather than their contingencies, affinities and dependencies.

Similarly, the feminist philosopher Donna Haraway has proposed a radical re-envisioning of the human subject as cyborg, which entails a rejection of dualistic concepts and embraces an ontology that incorporates human, animal and machine—a form of assemblage (Haraway 1991). In this model the cyborg is not the other but *us*, as heterogeneous, dynamic, and contingent entities that do not have stable or clear boundaries.

This evokes Heidegger's concept of *Dasein*, where the subject is understood as a nonautonomous and culturally bound entity, that is fluid, reconfiguring as a function of its relations with other things. Dasein expresses Heidegger's rejection of the Cartesian primacy of the self-sufficient subject;

> the distinction between an inner and an outer is constructive and continually gives occasion for further constructions, we shall in the future no longer speak of a subject, of a subjective sphere, but shall understand the being to whom intentional comportments belong as Dasein. (Heidegger BP: 64 in: Dreyfus 2010)

In her recent book *Unthought* (2017), Hayles further develops key ideas such as technogenesis, to propose a more distributed and less ontologically differentiated understanding of what cognition might be. Hayles's argument could be considered (arguably, erroneously) an augmentation of Marshall McLuhan's concept of *extensions of man* (McLuhan 1964). Whereas McLuhan considers technology as an augmentation or extension of the human, Hayles conceives of the relationships between people and technology as a co-evolving assemblage, each essential to the other's ontology. Hayles refers to these "complex interactions between human and nonhuman cognizers and their abilities to enlist material forces" (Hayles 2017: 115) as a *cognitive assemblage*. Acknowledging the importance of Bruno Latour's development of Actor Network Theory as foundational to her own thinking, Hayles proposes this cognitive assemblage as

> a particular kind of network, characterized by the circulation of information, interpretations, and meanings by human and technical cognizers who drop in and out of the network in shifting configurations that enable interpretations and meanings to emerge, circulate, interact and disseminate throughout the network. (Hayles 2019: 175)

This is not to equate human and nonhuman agency. Rather, Hayles highlights the interdependency of things with other things, an interdependency that contributes to how things come to be and are then sustained, recognising that these are not fixed but dynamic relations—each thing, in its continually motile relations, being in a continuously unstable and emergent state of becoming. Creative technologies researcher Oliver Bown has observed that some advanced technical systems employed in live music improvisation (e.g. that are sometimes referred to as 'virtual musicians') should not be confused with human capability, as "the implication is that these systems open up a new space of interactive performance that is not necessarily best grounded in comparisons with human behaviour" (Bown 2018: 38).

Related research and practice

The key aim in the *Double Agent* project was to explore how humans and machines could co-create an authentically affective environment that allows people (interactors) to visually and proprioceptively experience their enmeshment in, and as part of, the system. There has been prior research and development in this area. The work of Oliver Bown at the Interactive Media Lab at the University of New South Wales (UNSW), aims to facilitate creative engagement between human and machine-learning systems. The machine-learning system in a work such as *Zamyatin* (Bown 2018), is placed as a co-performer, an accompanying improviser, which enters a 'creative' dialogue with a human performer or performers.

The research and performance projects, *Recognition* and *Instrumental*, by a team of researchers from Deakin University (Motion.lab and Centre for Intelligent Systems Research) and Royal Melbourne Institute of Technology, offer us examples of two approaches to how a virtual performing agent might be deployed in a creative context. In *Recognition* the virtual agent learns specific sequences of dance movement and can stand in for a human interactor to animate an interactive projected avatar. By contrast, in *Instrumental* the agent is a performing partner, "able to recognize the dancers [sic] movement and synthesize movement sequences based on the human dancer's movements" (McCormick et al. 2015: 18). In both these works the machine-learning agent uses an Artificial Neural Network to learn sequences of movement from the human dancers, and is deployed in a similar manner to that in Bown's project—as a co-performer, rather than as an immersive and encapsulating element in a system where each element (humans and machines) might be conceptualised and experienced as an assemblage.

Petra Gemeinboeck (Creative Robotics Lab, National Institute for Experimental Arts, UNSW) and Rob Saunders (Design Lab, University of Sydney) have explored the affective potential of creative robotics, bringing together dance and machine-learning, to develop "a novel relational approach that harnesses dancers' movement expertise to design a nonanthropomorphic robot, its potential to move and capacity to learn" (Gemeinboeck/Saunders 2017: 1), using a methodology they call *Performative Body Mapping* (PBM). The initial stage of this process is *bodying*, in which the robot's form is developed as it learns about embodied movement from motion tracking data of dancers improvising within unusual costumes and prostheses, such as a cardboard cube and a broken tetrahedron. The subsequent machine-learning process involved in Gemeinboeck and Saunders' research is structured in three stages; *grounding, imitation* and *improvisation*, with the machine-learning system gathering data during the *grounding* phase from the robotic mechanism's physical interactions with its environment. During the *imitation* stage the machine-learning system acquires data by mirroring a dancer 'operating' a costume prosthesis. In the final *improvisation* phase "the machine learns to play with the movement material given to develop movements that are unique to its own machinic body and its relations to the environment" (ibid: 6).

Other research has focused on applying machine-learning to human movement, and particularly dance, as a tool for aiding the development of choreographic projects, rather than as the key element in a creative project. Important developments have been made in projects undertaken in collaboration with Google's Art & Culture Laboratory, led by Wayne McGregor and Bill T. Jones respectively, and the machine-learning based *Chor-rnn* system developed by Luka Crnkovic-Friis and Louise Crnkovic-Friis.

As described on the website *Experiments with Google*, the Google Arts & Culture Lab collaborated with choreographer Wayne McGregor to develop a *Living Archive*, a "creative tool, using machine-learning. Now, anyone, anywhere can take inspiration from McGregor's body of work to create their own piece of dance" (Girschig 2019). A key factor in this project is the massive scale of the database— almost half a million moments of movement from McGregor's 25 year archive— employed in the training of the machine-learning choreographic tool, which allows remote users, from the comfort of their own home, to "strike a pose" with their own webcam, search for closest matches in the database and then have the system "connect them together to create your own piece of choreography" (ibid). McGregor subsequently employed a more advanced version of this tool, trained on 100 hours of dance video footage of his dancers, to inform the choreographic development of the performance work *Living Archive: An AI Performance Experiment* (2019).

McGregor's initial experiments with AI, in 2004, aimed to develop "an independent dance entity [...] that could respond to and solve the kinds of choreographic tasks that he set for his dancers" (Leach/deLahunta 2017: 462). Collaborating with digital artists Marc Downie and Nick Rothwell, the *Choreographic Language Agent* (CLA) was developed as a software tool for use by McGregor in his own choreographic process, and by other dance makers, the prototype being "something more like an extended digital notebook" (ibid: 463).

Bill T. Jones's project *Body Movement Language* (2019) is a collection of experiments resulting from a two way residency between the choreographer and Google's Art & Culture Lab, inspired by the artist's long history of intertwining improvised speech and dance. The experiments use machine-learning to invite users to explore the creative possibilities of speech and movement and make new connections with Jones's work, using their laptop computer connected to the internet, integrating the dancer's movement with dynamic rendering of text.

The *Chor-rnn* system, developed by Luka Crnkovic-Friis (Peltarion) and Louise Crnkovic-Friis (The Lulu Art Group), employs recent advances in deep learning to make novel computer generated choreography (Crnkovic-Friis/Crnkovic-Friis 2016). The system uses a deep recurrent neural network, trained on motion capture data of contemporary dancers, which can generate new sequences. This generated material is displayed as an animated stick figure, from which one can learn and execute novel movement in the choreographic language style of the work it was trained on. As such the system might be used "as a creativity catalyst or choreographic partner" (ibid: 276).

There are other significant examples of machine-learning applied to the interpretation and generation of creative human movement that might be discussed here, such as historically important work by Merce Cunningham, or the recent work of the UK artistic duo Igloo (briefly referred to later as Gibson/Martelli), but this discussion is not aiming to provide an exhaustive review of activity in the field. Other more extensive publications can provide a broader view of the field (e.g.: Bleeker 2017; Audry 2021). Rather, our focus is on the ideas and questions that motivated the development of the *Double Agent* project. A key consideration that arises here concerns how we have approached the question of creativity.

The question of creativity

In the *Double Agent* project the question of creative agency is paramount. Any discussion of creativity requires an appreciation of what the term might mean. Anthropologist James Leach employs the term to describe cultural practices where the creation of new things, and the forms of exchange enacted around them, function to create individuals and bind them in social groups, creating the community they inhabit (Leach 2013). Leach suggests that creativity exists as dynamic cultural relations that create people and things. He considers creativity as far more than a motivating factor in the making of cultural artefacts (where we anticipate creativity as a defining characteristic), but as a property that pervades human society and subsequent human behaviour. Human relationships, with one another and their environment (both manufactured and natural), are seen as negotiated, nurtured and realized—*created*. Further to this, these foundational aspects of human societal behaviour are considered by Leach as innately creative and from which other forms of creativity arise. In this context we can inquire as to what manner of generative dynamics (creativity) operate when the relationships are between humans and autonomous machines? Our aim in the *Double Agent* project has been to develop an environment where human and nonhuman agents co-create a generative assemblage of which they are each a part.

Following Leach's argument, creativity might be considered a distributed phenomenon, emergent from communities, collectives and assemblages, driving change that can result in individual and collective social formation. Cognitive scientist David Kirsh describes distributed creativity, in the domain of dance, as "the mechanisms by which team members harness resources to *interactively invent* concepts and elements, and then structure things into a coherent product" (Kirsh 2011: 141). Whilst collective creativity can be focused on the object as outcome, it can also form the distributed subject. In this case creative agency is not considered a property of things (either human or nonhuman) but as what anthropologist Lucy Suchman (2008) has described as relational effects which are emergent from varying arrangements and interactions of human and nonhuman elements.

Such social interactions are increasingly mediated by technologies with enhanced degrees of agency. Machine-learning is the capacity of a computational system to learn structure (patterns) from data in order to make predictions (further patterns) on new data. Social media platforms and search engines learn our preferences, and smart surveillance systems recognise our behaviour.

This entangling of human and machine can be observed in what Suchman has described as a sociality of machines, where AI is developed as a metaphor of biosocial evolution (ibid), prefiguring Hayles' concept of technogenesis. Through such techno-human assemblage (e.g. prostheses, drones, interactive environments) a novel form of hybrid human and nonhuman subjectivity might be seen to emerge, enmeshing distributed cognition and networked agency.

The proposition in *Double Agent*, is that creativity can be considered as emergent from the interactions of people and machines in the form of sociotechnical co-creation and that the outcomes of that process can generate cognitive assemblages which manifest that creativity.

Double Agent

Simon Biggs developed the concept for the *Double Agent* project and wrote the software applications that underpin the work. Samya Bagchi developed the machine-learning model employed in the project, supervised by Mark McDonnell. Sue Hawksley led the choreographic aspects of the project and collaborated with dancer Tammy Arjona to iteratively develop the movement material used in the machine-learning model.

The *Double Agent* project was initially developed to explore the multiple modalities of agency in the moving (dancing) body. The focus was on maximising the interactors' proprioceptive sense of their immersion in and interaction with a software generated agent, so as to enhance their sense of their own agency, through their effect within, and the affect of, the environment. In its earlier iterations the work was composed as a single large scale projected display (approximately 6 x 3.5 metres) featuring an emergent 'virtual agent', which was visualised as a highly responsive 'structure' emerging from the interactions of thousands of invisible software objects with the interactors who inhabit the installation space. This element of *Double Agent* can be seen as the silver coloured (lower) imagery in Figure 2 (below).

As the project developed, a second projected display was incorporated, running as a separate software application but in constant communication with the original *Double Agent* application. This second element employs the machine-learning, and computational representation, of human movement to create a 'machine-learning agent' (visible as the upper, golden imagery in Figure 2). This agent can observe and respond to the interactors, as well as to the behaviour of the emergent virtual agent (the lower, silver imagery), to create an environment composed as distinct qualia of distributed agency.

Fig. 2: *Double Agent*, 2018, Simon Biggs, interactive installation, Museum of Discovery, Adelaide, Australia. Performer Sue Hawksley. (image: Simon Biggs)

Double Agent is an interactive augmented environment where people physically interact with a virtual agent, which is an emergent phenomenon, rather than a distinct software entity, determined by the behaviour of thousands of small invisible software objects. These exist within a three-dimensional virtual space that incorporates a physics engine, and are thus subject to simulated physical laws (primarily those of fluid dynamics). The virtual objects are programmed to be both drawn to and repelled by the movement of human bodies in the installation space, similar to a flocking particle system. Each object is algorithmically encapsulated, employing object oriented programming (OOP) protocols, and possesses various properties and behaviours, such as being attracted to the moving joints of the motion tracking acquired three-dimensional model of the interactors within the installation space as well as being repelled by other similar objects and, when in overly close proximity, the simulated joints of the interactors. For each object this creates an oppositional dynamic that has to be resolved through finding an equilibrium between the competing forces. At any moment thousands of such objects are doing this, unseen by the interactors, creating an immersive fluidly dynamic environment of potential energy.

The virtual agent is formed from the totality of this behaviour as a complex, emergent, three-dimensional visual 'structure'. The structure is composed of graphic vectors that are drawn between the invisible objects as they come into closer proximity and alignment with one another. The objects are aware of each other and exchange messages, causing the connecting vectors to be drawn when the appropriate conditions are satisfied. This is often a fleeting event, the vector appearing like a flash of lightning. At other times the vector is sustained for an extended period of time, along with other vectors, creating the impression of a tensile, fluid but relatively stable visual structure—the agent as a singular entity. However, this is an emergent higher level illusion, an illusion that nevertheless functions as if it were a single agent and, in the manner it does so, evokes questions as to whether we, the interactor, might be similarly emergent and heterogeneous, an unstable and contingent assemblage?

Engagement with the virtual agent encourages the human interactors to explore the system's tensional polarities and the sense of physical extension and diffusion it allows. It is the tensegrity and elasticity in the structure, along with the immediacy of interaction and immersion, that affects the kinetic/kinesthetic sense, and which has been reported by dancers and others who have interacted with the *Double Agent* system. Dancer Tammy Arjona said,

you feel sometimes like you're not just living in the body you have, that there's an extension of you, and there's bits of you out there and its constantly trying to refind 'you' and gathering in, but always you're sort of leaking out a little bit (laughs). It's a bit like we weren't on earth, we were on another planet or something, and our form is not the form that it usually is, that you're actually more dispersed, there's bits of you that could be anywhere at one time but it's always trying to come back to the central core [...] you don't have the edges of you. (Personal communication, 2016)

Tammy also noted that she experienced a feeling of haptic resistance in the virtual space; "it definitely changes the texture of the space, maybe that 'thickness', sometimes it feels thicker, there's more weight, more thickness to the air, almost, because you've got this expanding and contracting thing" (ibid).

This correlates with Sita Popat's observation that despite us conceptually understanding that virtual worlds do not offer physical feedback, research in cognitive neuroscience demonstrates that our bodily memories facilitate our capacity to respond 'as if real', to 'flesh out' the sense of presence in the absence of substance when interacting in virtual reality environments (2017). Reporting on her experience of Gibson/Martelli's VR work *White Island* (2014) Popat noted,

My body became blurred, existing between the definable points of physical and virtual, so that the experience of the environment was 'not not real' [...] The space was neither corporeal nor virtual, since it was defined by my body's deep proprioceptive knowledge colouring the virtual world with shades of physical experience. (Popat 2017)

Two fold Agency

The title *Double Agent*, intends to evoke the twofold agency of the work, wherein a computationally emergent virtual agent interacts with a live interactor, whilst a machine-learning agent simultaneously 'dances' based on what it has learned from recorded motion tracking data of the dancers improvising and interacting within the *Double Agent* environment. The process of acquiring this data was a teaching and learning process for both the machine-learning agent and the dance artists who spent many hours within the interactive environment to develop their understanding of the particular dynamics of the virtual elements and the environment.

The invisible objects that underpin the emergent system are attracted to the presence of the dancers (both human and that generated by the machine-learning system), but repelled by their movement. The reaction is relative to the dynamics and vectors of the dancers' movement, which generates latent energy in the objects. This affects both the attraction and repulsion, as the former involves the application of a force inverse to that generated by the collisions and ricochets between the objects with one another and the rigid body representations of the dancers in the physics engine. Consequently, these conflicting tensions within the system inform the dancers choices, employing both visual and proprioceptive judgement (often unconsciously), and thus their movement behaviour.

Stillness and micromovements, which generate little energy, can allow the virtual agent to gather closely around the body, creating what feels, to the dancers, to be a meshlike organism in which delicate, subtle movements cause small febrile quivers of disturbance. Moving at speed and traversing the space scatters the objects; slowing or stilling allows them to regroup, like magnets drawn back to the body. But if they have been thrown far and wide (sometimes to the extent that they are all flung beyond our view of the virtual world, leaving the projected image empty of vectors), this regrouping can take a considerable time, as the objects orbit like comet tails or spiral nebula, gradually returning to centre upon the body or bodies. Repeatedly crossing the space toward and away from the Kinect movement sensor (located below the screen) generates 'waves', rather like the dancer carrying a full bowl of (virtual) water. Once invested with energy, the rocking of the waves takes time to settle long after the interactors have stopped moving, or leaves traces of the waves echoing in whatever behaviour the system adopts as the interactors proceed to their next activity.

If two or more interactors occupy the interactive space, the vectors appear to seek a centre that is equidistant between them, not dissimilar to a trojan asteroid seeking its Lagrange point amongst larger masses. The phenomenon is emergent from the application of an inverse force to each individual object along a vector between it and, from frame to frame, a randomly selected joint from a randomly selected person in the interactive environment. The outcome is that the objects swarm (invisibly) around the joints of all the interactors, creating an averaging (and thus centering) effect. When objects come into proximity to one another their relationship is visualised as a fleeting line drawn between them. It is only this latter, emergent, phenomenon that is visible to the interactors in the environment, but such minimal means are sufficient to create a strong sense of immersion in a highly reactive fluid and tensile structure. The dancers reported that the experience of interacting in *Double Agent* raised their awareness of the impact of their presence in, and on, an environment, and the disturbance caused by being there.

In *Double Agent* no body is displayed; rather the interactors' somatic experience of the effect of their presence on the virtual material brings the invisible body to attention. Interestingly, in Wayne McGregor's *Choreographic Language Agent* project mentioned earlier, the prototype was little used. The interface allowed users to draw, shift and link points, lines and planes in 3D space using a keyboard, mouse and screen, but this felt cumbersome and more of an impediment than an affordance to the choreographic process. The dancers and McGregor observed that "it really needs a body" (Leach/deLahunta 2017: 464). Based on the realisation that the body "has presence, and that presence has an effect", Downie and Rothwell developed a new choreographic entity, *Becoming*, on the platform of the CLA software. Although still an abstract form and not an obvious representation of a human body, *Becoming* was designed to be "an aesthetically and kinesthetically compelling presence" (ibid: 465). Leach and deLahunta comment that "to be with this strange entity is to feel something of the capacity of bodies to elicit response" (ibid), and for McGregor it became a compelling "11th dancer" in his choreographic process (ibid).

In *Double Agent*, the dance is more about the relationship between the invisible body and the felt qualities of the dancers' interaction with the virtual material. Dancer Sue Hawksley said,

I wasn't acting as a puppeteer; it felt like we were immersed and enmeshed in material that could not be precisely controlled, which determined aspects of our range and choice of activity and stillness, and demanded the patience to allow the system to 'do its own thing'. (Personal communication, 2017)

Once the dancers became accustomed to the interactive environment they continued improvising within it, but with their movement data being recorded and saved for use in the machine-learning process (as described below). Particular movement choices that emerged from the improvisations were the repeating of actions and patterns, periods of patiently waiting to allow time for responses, and an emphasis on spatial rather than bodily and skeletal movement. Learning from this, the machine-learning agent is enabled to make its own movement choices which, whilst uncannily similar to the dancers', consist of a host of novel moves—this includes teleporting from position to position without transition, flying through space and having appendages of indeterminate length and an elastic quality—superhuman actions that could be interpreted as a form of (self) creative agency emergent from the machine-learning process. The interactive virtual environment of *Double Agent* might be considered a world where simulated 'natural' laws allow a v-zombie to exist and dance.

The outcome is the emergence of a software generated co-performer, or co-interactor, that cohabits the installation space with the human interactors and contributes to the collective construction and experience of the artwork that subsequently emerges. Like a ghostly dancer in the machine, this machine-learning agent is 'aware' of its immediate environment, monitoring the level of activity of the human interactors in the space and conditioning its own behaviour as an inverse correlate—the more active the human interactors the less active the machine-learning agent and, inversely, the less active the human interactors the more active the machine-learning agent (although, when the work was later exhibited at the Movement and Computing Conference in Arizona this correlate was inverted, so the dynamics of the machine-learning agent more or less mirrored that of the performer, dancer Ziqian Zhou).

The intention in all this is not to create a dancing ghost or zombie. Rather, the installation, the software, computers, sensors and interactors (both human and computer generated) are intended to exist as a contingent assemblage that, from moment to moment and state to state, instantiates itself as a dynamic heterogeneous subject.

The Machine-Learning Agent

As might be understood from the title *Double Agent*, there is more than one level, or fold, of agency active in the work. The machine-learning generated agent incorporated within the system is an entity that has independently learned how to 'dance' employing the machine-learning method known as a Long Short-Term Memory Recurrent Neural Network (LSTM-RNN) (Hochreiter/Schmidhuber 1997). LSTM-RNNs allow computational systems to evolve models of complex behaviour, such as human movement. The system learns to predict the future based on historical data, which in our case are dance patterns. Our goal was to generate novel dance patterns by iteratively feeding back the predicted dance movement at a specific time instance to its history and use it as a seed to predict the next dance movement. This section provides a short technical description of how this work was realized.

The original dance motion was recorded using a commercially available Microsoft Kinect sensor Version 2. The Kinect sensor represents the human body as a set of 3D coordinates, using 25 discrete joints, and a capture rate of 25 Hz. The sensor is capable of tracking six distinct human bodies at one time.

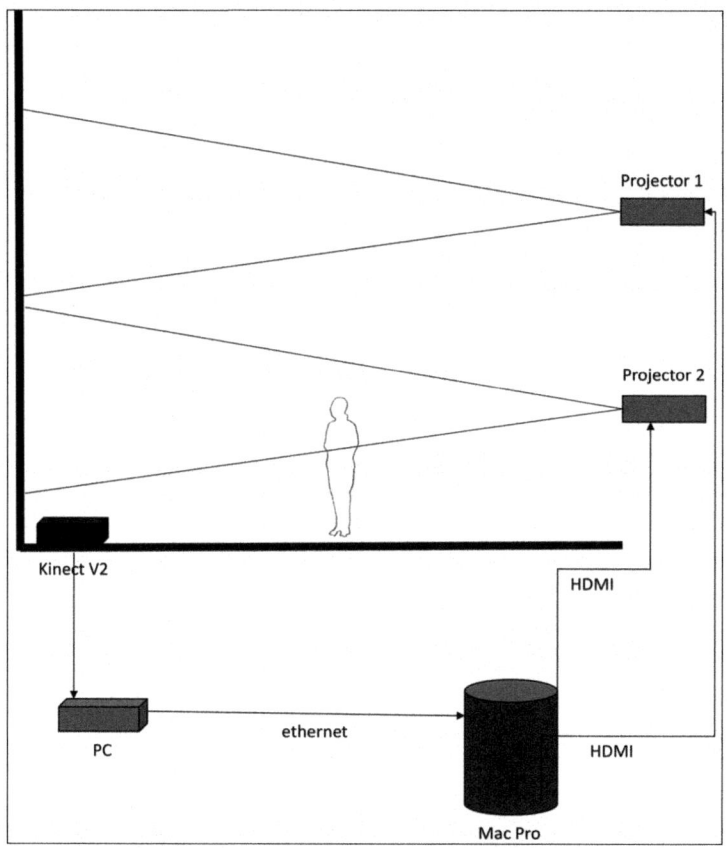

Fig. 3: Flow diagram of Double Agent installation components.

A Processing software application written by Simon Biggs was running on a Windows 10 laptop, to acquire the raw data from the Kinect, and to parse and save this data in a format suitable for the machine-learning algorithm. This is the same application that provides the live stream of Kinect data, over a network connection, to two other programs (also written in Processing, and running simultaneously on the same Mac Pro desktop computer, with two different immersive projection displays connected) that generate the live visual agents which respond, respectively, to the interactors and the machine-learning generated agent (see Figure 3, above and Figure 4, below).

The dataset acquired from the live dancers and employed in the training of the machine-learning agent consists of eight hours of original and unique dance data made up of sequences of improvised dance movements. Each sequence features a single dancer (either Sue or Tammy) with the duration of the sequences varying between six to ten minutes.

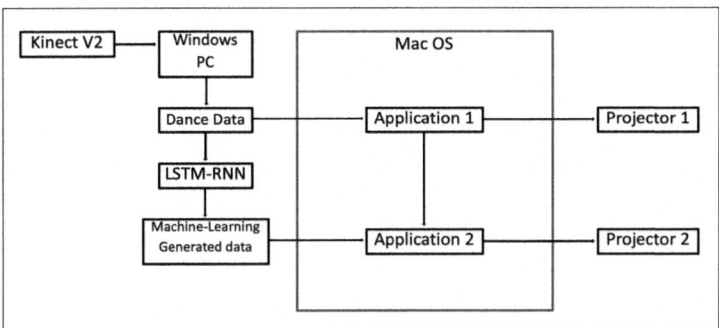

Fig. 4: Functional Flow Diagram of Double Agent

Since any subset of a dance sequence is also a valid dance sequence (given the indiscrete nature of human movement) we exploit this to generate a larger training dataset of 48 hours by creating numerous new sequences with random starting points. The duration of each of the obtained sequences was set at fifteen seconds. We used the first ten seconds of the sequence as initial input and the last five seconds as the supervised output. Each second we take 25 frames and, as each frame has 25 joints expressed as a 3D coordinate, our data can be represented using a 75 x 375 matrix. The LSTM-RNN employed in our experiments is trained using the Tensorflow deep learning framework .

For generating new sequences, the model requires a seed input of 10 seconds of dance data. In our case, we give the recorded dance data as input, which needs to be normalized. The generated sequence is then denormalized using the corresponding min-max value. Generating a longer continuous sequence requires appending each of the generated sequences, allowing the creation of larger sets of generated dance data, typically around 10 to 20MB of numerical data (eg: x,y,z timestamped joint coordinates) for any specific sequence. The final result allows for generated dance data sequences, each several minutes in duration, to be employed to create a machine-learning agent, that is then deployed as skeleton data—a 'little man' or homunculus—in the interactive *Double Agent* environment, along with the live Kinect acquired skeletons of other (human) interactors. Although the figure is not visibly displayed the actions of this machine-learning agent are apparent in its interaction within its own object/vector environment (running in application 2), leading to the emergence of the gold and silver coloured tensile and fluid visual structures that emerges from human interaction in the installation space.

Conclusion

Double Agent seeks to explore the liminal and transgressive augmentation of human and nonhuman agency, offering a scenario where creativity and authorship operate across distributed systems involving human and nonhuman agents, evoking a continuing cyborg evolution with ourselves embedded at the centre of this process.

As described here, the work includes the development of a software generated co-interactor—a machine-learning agent—that cohabits the installation space with human interactors, contributing to the collective construction and experience of the work. Ironically (since the following proposition is as far removed from the ideas that motivated the *Double Agent* project as can be imagined), this machine-learning agent might be considered to resemble the 'ghost' of the dualist model of cognition, a tiny version of ourselves, within our mind, with executive control over cognitive and other functions. In *Double Agent* the machine-learning agent is formed as an invisible 'little man', with its own agency and immersed in an environment that is a correlate of the interactive environment the people in the *Double Agent* installation inhabit. This presents us with precisely the problem Ryle identified when he described the fallacy of the 'ghost in the machine'.

However, in *Double Agent* the dancers, actual and virtual, are involved in a more nuanced and enmeshed relationship with the other elements in the installation assemblage. In addition to learning to negotiate its own environment, the machine-learning agent monitors the activity of human interactors and conditions its own behaviour in response, entering into an improvised process of exchange where human and machine are entangled as an assemblage.

Double Agent seeks to problematise the role of agency within complex distributed systems, whether human, machine or hybrid. In this context the dualism critiqued by Ryle is clearly unsustainable—although that was an easy target. So too, Chalmer's p-zombie thought experiment can be considered irrelevant, it's logic dependent on a false dualism that in *Double Agent* is denied, in favour of a heterogeneous and contingent, but nevertheless relatively stable, assemblage. Haraway's proposed cyborg, melding human and nonhuman elements, and especially Hayles's concept of cognitive assemblage, would appear the closer correlates to what *Double Agent* manifests; an example of Hayles' technogenesis in action, with human and machine viscerally enmeshed in its evolving performance. In *Double Agent* there is no singular 'dancer in the machine'. The system as a whole, where human and nonhuman agents co-create a generative assemblage of which they are each a part, is the dancer.

References

Audry, Sofian (2021): Art in the Age of Machine Learning, Cambridge: MIT Press.

Biggs, Simon (2018): "Double Agent". Retrieved from http://littlepig.org.uk/installations/doubleagent/index.htm on February 29, 2022.

Biggs, Simon/Hawksley, Sue/Paine, Garth (2014): "Crosstalk: Making People in Interactive Spaces." In: Proceedings of the International Workshop on Movement and Computing (MOCO '14), Paris, France: ACM, pp. 61-65.

Biggs, Simon/Hawksley, Sue/Paine, Garth (2016): "Bodytext: somatic data as agency in interactive dance." In: Carla. Fernandez (ed.), Multimodality and Performance, Newcastle, UK: Cambridge Scholars Publishing, pp. 179-186.

Bleeker, Maaike (2017): Transmission in Motion: the technologizing of dance, Oxford: Routledge.

Bown, Oliver (2018): "Performer interaction and expectation with live algorithms: experiences with 'Zamyatin'." In: Digital Creativity, 29(1), pp. 37-50.

Chalmers, David (1996): The Conscious Mind, New York: Oxford University Press.

Crnkovic-Friis, Luka/Crnkovic-Friis, Louise (2016): "Generative Choreography using Deep Learning." In: Proceedings of the 7th International Conference on Computational Creativity, (ICCC2016), Paris, France: Sony CSL, pp. 272-277.

Dreyfus, Hubert L. (2010): "Heidegger and Foucault on the Subject, Agency and Practices." Department of Philosophy archives, University of California, Berkeley. Retrieved from https://web.archive.org/web/20061214215014/http://ist-socrates.berkeley.edu/~hdreyfus/html/paper_heidandfoucault.html on February 8, 2022.

Gemeinboeck, Petra/Saunders, Rob (2017): "Movement Matters: How a Robot Becomes Body." In: Proceedings of the 4th International Conference on Movement Computing (MOCO '17), New York, NY, USA: ACM, pp. 8:1-8:8.

Girschig, Bastien (2019): "Experiments with Google: Living Archive by Wayne McGregor." Retrieved from https://experiments.withgoogle.com/living-archive-wayne-mcgregor on January 19, 2022.

Haraway, Donna (1991): Simians, Cyborgs and Women: The Reinvention of Nature, New York: Routledge.

Hayles, N. Katherine (2012): How We Think: Digital Media and Contemporary Technogenesis, Chicago: University of Chicago Press.

Hayles, N. Katherine (2017): Unthought: The Power of the Cognitive Nonconscious, Chicago: University of Chicago Press.

Hayles, N. Katherine (2019): "Literary Texts as Cognitive Assemblages: The Case of Electronic Literature." Interface Critique Journal, 2, pp. 173–195.

Hochreiter, Sepp/Schmidhuber, Jürgen (1997): "Long Short-Term Memory." Neural Computation, 9(8), pp. 1735-80.

Jones, Bill T. (2019): "Body, Movement, Language: AI Sketches with Bill T. Jones." Retrieved from https://experiments.withgoogle.com/billtjonesai on January 19, 2022.

Kingma, Diederik/Ba, Jimmy (2015): "Adam: A method for stochastic optimization." In: Proceedings of the 3rd International Conference on Learning Representations (ICLR, 2015), San Diego, CA, USA. Retrieved from https://arxiv.org/abs/1412.6980v5 on February 12, 2022.

Kirsh, David (2011): "Creative Cognition in Choreography." In: Proceedings of the 2nd International Conference on Computational Creativity. (ICCC 2011), Mexico City, Mexico, pp. 141-146.

Leach, James (2003): Creative Land: Place and procreation of the Rai Coast of Papua New Guinea, New York: Berghahn Books.

Leach, James/deLahunta, Scott (2017): "Dance 'Becoming' Knowledge: designing a digital 'body'." Leonardo, 50(5), pp. 461–467.

McCormick, John/Hutchison, Steph/Nash, Adam/Vincs, Kim/Nahavandi, Saeid/Creighton, Douglas (2015): "Recognition: Combining Human Interaction and a Digital Performing Agent." International Journal of Virtual Reality, 15(1), pp. 18-24.

McGregor, Wayne (2019): "Living Archive: An AI Performance Experiment." Retrieved from https://waynemcgregor.com/productions/living-archive on January 19, 2022.

McLuhan, Marshall (1964): Understanding Media: The Extensions of Man, Canada: McGraw-Hill.

Popat, Sita (2017): "Virtually Touching: Embodied engagement in telematic and virtual reality performance." White Rose University Consortium online repository [accepted version of a book chapter published in: Jo Butterworth/Liesbeth Wildschut (eds.) Contemporary Choreography: A Critical Reader. London: Routledge, pp. 480-491]. Retrieved from http://eprints.whiterose.ac.uk/125649/ on February 8, 2022.

Ryle, Gilbert (2009): The Concept of Mind (60th Anniversary edition), London: Routledge.

Suchman, Lucy (2008): Plans and Situated Actions: the problem of Human Machine Communication, Cambridge: Cambridge University Press.

Xu, Bing/Wang, Naiyan/Chen, Tianqi/Li, Mu (2015): "Empirical Evaluation of Rectified Activations in Convolutional Network." In: Proceedings of the 3rd International Conference on Learning Representations (ICLR, 2015). arXiv preprint. Retrieved from: https://arxiv.org/abs/1505.00853 on February 12, 2022.

History and Theory of Algorithmic Art

Web Search Fever and Collecting as the Human Condition

Patricia de Vries

Abstract

According to theorists of media and technology we live in an algorithmic culture. Algorithms shape, organise and co-produce everyday life in ways that vary from the seemingly quotidian to the heavily politicised, has given academics and artists anxieties about the future of algorithmic culture in light of these developments. Some types of algorithms garner more attention than others. Web search is a recurring topic of concern both in art and academia. And for good reason. Search engines form a key part of the infrastructure of online information. How are we to better understand this seemingly mundane activity? Camille Henrot's experimental film Grosse Fatigue (2013) frames web search as a form of collecting and refers to Walter Benjamin's conceptualisation of the collector. I argue that Grosse Fatigue offers a choreography not just on the centralised, monetised and monopolised structures of Google's search engine, but on the act of collecting as the human condition.

Keywords

algorithms, art, web search, anxiety, collector, Walter Benjamin, Camille Henrot, Google, recursion, self-referentiality.

We will wander, improvise, fall short and move in circles

J. HALBERSTAM (2011

Introduction

If theorists of media and technology are to be believed, we live in an algorithmic culture (Galloway 2006; Striphas 2015; Dourish 2016). Ted Striphas describes this developing algorithmic culture as a "shift" that first began 30 years ago, as humans increasingly started to delegate "the work of culture—the sorting, classifying and hierarchising of people, places, objects and ideas—to computational processes" (Striphas 2015: 395). Aspects of everyday life are increasingly delegated to algorithms and accompanied by an algorithmic type of rationality (e.g. Halpern

2014). The claim that algorithms shape, organise and co-produce everyday life in ways that vary from the seemingly quotidian to the heavily politicised, has also given impetus to anxieties about the present and future of algorithmic culture in light of these developments.

Some types of algorithms garner more attention than others. Web search anxiety is a recurring topic of concern both in art *and* academia, resulting in outstanding work on aspects of web search. Various scholars from a variety of disciplines have expressed concern in particular about the monopolisation of Google search (e.g. Jordan 2015; Couldry 2012; Fuchs 2012; Gehl 2014; Epstein 2019) and on the capitalist rationality behind Google's search engine (e.g. Mager 2012; Lewandowski 2014; Campanelli 2014; Jarrett 2014; Jordan 2015). Astrid Mager, for example, has written about how the algorithms behind search engines are shaped by their for-profit target-advertising business-models and advance a capitalist logic and ideology (Mager, 2012). Wendy Chun argues that software and hardware are "ideology machines" (Chun 2006: 19). Further, issues of globalisation and localisation of web browsers used in different fields and geolocations have flourished too (e.g. Jiang 2012; Jobin/Glassey 2014; Vaidhyanathan 2011; Petzold 2011; Pariser 2011), as well as reflections on past and present search technologies and their implementations (e.g. Knight/Mercer 2015; Ørmen 2014, 2016). Significant work has been done on the political and cultural bias reflected in search results (e.g. Dutton et al. 2017; Epstein/Robertson 2015; Hoffman 2019). Safiya Umoja Noble shows in *Algorithms of Oppression: How Search Engines Reinforce Racism* (2018) how Google's search engine "reflects the political, social, and cultural values of the society that search engines operate within," including the racist and sexist beliefs of the society (2018: 148). Research on the legal implications of search engines has grown, too (e.g. Becker/Stadler 2010). Taina Bucher sums it up thus: search algorithms hint at the "fundamental question of who or what has the power to set the conditions for what can be seen and known with whatever possible effects" (Bucher 2018: 3-4).

Search anxiety stretches beyond Google's search engine. What underpins of these anxieties and why web search forms the subject of critique is rarely interrogated, less so when this criticism takes the form of an artistic portrayal, which is what this paper will address. How web search is imagined, represented, and narrativised in art, can also be understood as an effect of web search in and of itself. Artworks are sites of meaning on which ideas and stories about algorithms are circulated, stretched, organised, and shaped. Focusing on an artistic portrayal of web search takes us away from questions revolving around what, when, and where search algorithms are to shift attention to the idea that web search "does" something beyond its technical capabilities. This paper engages specifically with the anxieties that Google's search engine evokes. The point of departure is the observation that web search is an addressee of concern in public debate, academic disciplines, and contemporary art. It focuses on Google primarily because it is the most used search engine, at least in Europe and the U.S. The entanglement of human beings in the for-profit algorithmic networks of this company has become a matter of concern for artists and critics alike.

Artistic Imaginaries of Google Search

Elizabeth Kolbert observes: "Thirty years ago, almost no one used the internet for anything. Today, just about everybody [in the West] uses it for everything" (Kolbert 2017). Thirty years ago, some hoped that the internet would weaken information monopolies by offering inclusive access to information on the web. Things turned out differently. Managing the complex information infrastructures of the internet has come with user reliance on search engines. Search engines form a key part of the infrastructure of online information. Or rather and more to the point, "surfing the web" in the West has come with reliance on Google's search engine. In popular perception, and absent strong competition, Google is perceived as *the* archive of the web, and even as *the web*—and "googling" has become close to synonymous with a web search. Its engine is assumed to comprise all current information on the internet and offers many other related information products through its many services. The company is also one of the largest computer manufacturers in the world. To service its users, it makes use of massive storage and computing power it manufactures itself. Google's competitive advantage is further reflected in the Oxford English Dictionary. "To google" was added as a verb to the O.E.D. in 2006, meaning to "search for information about (someone or something) on the internet using the search engine Google" (Google). The verb's common currency reflects Google's stable market share of over 90%. It also reflects its commercially- and technically-centralised position. Due to Google's high search volume and market share, an industry of marketeers continually tries to manipulate Google's algorithms to improve their ranking in Google's search engine. How is this reliance on Google's information infrastructure perceived by artists, and what anxieties are braided around Google's centralised position?

Google's monopoly position is also a cause of anxiety for artists. Much academic work is dedicated to showing how web search mediated by Google is imbricated in a system that thinks merely in terms of profits and what the implications are thereof. Here, issues arise that have to do with the use of personal data, the for-profit logic behind search algorithms, and the power imbalance therein. Artistic work, on the other hand, tends to focus on specific algorithmic features that are part of the infrastructure of a web search. Anja Groten developed the *Machina Recordatio* (2013). In this alternative search engine, one can browse for specific topics and keywords relating to existential issues and romantic problems one may not want to share with Google. The search "results" have the form of voice recordings of elderly people giving life advice to searchers who want to keep their private lives somewhat private. Relatedly, Harlo Holmes and Camille Henrot created an offline *I Ching*-like search application named *Desktopmance* (2015), which algorithmically answers a user's personal questions about life decisions and the future with a poetic response based on a selection of poems liked by Holmes and Henrot, combined with images randomly selected from the files stored on the user's desktop. *Image Atlas* (2012), made by Taryn Simon in collaboration with Aaron Swartz, responds to anxiety about filter bubbles. The two developed a search engine that compares the top image results for search terms across localised engine settings of 57 countries worldwide. *Image Atlas*, in the artists' own words, "questions the supposed innocence and neutrality of the algorithms upon which search engines rely" (Simon 2012). To counter the self-referentiality of Google's search results, Phil Jones and Aharon Amir created the *Narcissus Search Engine for N.E.W.S.* (2009). Like Google's engine, *Narcissus* searches a database of documents for matching keywords, keeping tabs on when searchers click through to see the results. Contrary to Google's engine, it favours the less popular or unpopular over the popular. It does so by downplaying popular sites by pushing a popular result site down in its ranking. If a popular site continues to be clicked on despite these efforts, it will no longer appear in the list of results.

Artistic reflections on Google's search engines and algorithms comes in many guises. From iconic fictional browser narratives (Olia Lialina), a live stream of an artist's browser in real-time (Jonas Lund), a play with bots used to identify pornography on the internet (Jake Elwes), subversive play in the form of Google browser extensions (RedNoise), tinkering with Google's ad algorithms (Alessandro Ludovico), with its image search algorithms (Rebecca Lieberman), or with Google Chrome plug-ins (Rafael Roozendaal) to a physical theatrical performance piece in which a group enacts a search engine (Christophe Bruno). With these artistic interventions, artists tackle different aspects of search anxiety.

The acclaimed artist Camille Henrot has conducted one particularly insightful artwork on web search anxiety. In her experimental video *Grosse Fatigue* (2013), the emphasis goes to searching as an act of collecting, and it addresses the question of what constitutes a web search and why this is a cause of anxiety. To answer this question, the artist explores a long tradition of philosophical reflections on the will to know, zooming in on collecting as an activity that gives form to this desire. Her work reflects on the 'searching condition' of humans, the different modalities in which the quest for answers takes place and what underpins the quest for knowledge. Further, it reflects on what it means when this seemingly eternal search for answers is delegated to proprietary algorithms run by companies whose operations are based on the quest for profit. In the following, I focus on how *Grosse Fatigue* imagines search anxiety. What structures of feeling underlie web search? What is the connection between searching and storytelling?

Unlocking the World in Grosse Fatigue

Henrot's *Grosse Fatigue* loosely links religion and science, facts and emotions, and world-building to Google's search engine. Moreover, the artistic enactment of the act of collecting presented in *Grosse Fatigue* shows a way to work with and through the self-referentiality and recursiveness of Google's search engine. *Grosse Fatigue* carries its viewers through the realms of epistemology, taxonomy, theology, and technology, offering reflections on the act of collecting on the one hand and an artistic imaginary of the underlying moods and shapes of the quest for knowledge on the other.

Set entirely on a desktop computer, *Grosse Fatigue* begins with a window popping up on a desktop with the query "the history of the universe" being typed into the Google search bar. From there, the film takes its viewers on an audiovisual *tour de force*, along with numerous creation stories, down the rabbit hole of Google's web browser and through the collections of the Smithsonian Institute in Washington, D.C. In 13 minutes, the film covers millions of years in the history of the universe, crossing numerous disciplines, methods of research, and fields of expertise. *Grosse Fatigue* was made during Henrot's stint as a research fellow at the Smithsonian Institute in Washington D.C.—the world's largest conglomerate of museums and research centres administered by the U.S. government and holds over 137 million artworks, objects, and specimens in its collection. Her book, *Elephant Child* (2016), expands on some of the formative ideas for *Grosse Fatigue*. *Elephant Child* is partly a collection of the research material and thinking that informed *Grosse Fatigue* and offers images of the artworks and quotes of thinkers that have shaped Henrot's ideas.

Furthermore, Henrot connects the quotidian practice of web browsing to the eternal question of life on earth and the moods and shapes underlying the mystery of life on planet earth. Spirals and rectangles, hands, turtles, and globes reappear throughout the film as it draws in on the concepts of recursion, self-similarity and self-referentiality. To trace the connection between these concepts is to discern Henrot's understanding of what we do when we search.

Grosse Fatigue invites viewers to rethink the idea of a web search as broadly situated in the history of how knowledge is conceived, narrativised, preserved, distributed, and, importantly, *collected*. The footage of *Grosse Fatigue* consists of film images taken at the Smithsonian Institution combined with images and clips taken from Google Image and Google search results. The Smithsonian Institution is not modest about its ambitions. Its mission is to "unlock the mysteries of the universe" and to continue to take the

lead in the quest to understand the fundamental nature of the cosmos, using next-generation technologies to explore our own solar system, meteorites, the Earth's geological past and present, and the paleontological record of our planet (Smithsonian Institution).

Google has similar ambitions in the digital realm by, as one example, allowing its users to navigate the earth. Through Google Earth, one can traverse oceans and mountains or zoom in and out of cities. With Google Books, one can leaf through any of the books it has digitised, while Google Scholar provides access to the digital archives of museums and institutions, amongst other things. With its combined services and products, the company aims to "organise the world's information and make it universally accessible and useful" (Google Mission). In this sense, the Smithsonian Institute and the Google search engine would seem to be good places for starting a query on the universe's history. That said, queries into Google's vast database or the Smithsonian collection are mediated and governed queries. What Google's search algorithms and the Smithsonian have in common are their attempts to organise disorder.

The opening scene of *Grosse Fatigue* starts with an image of a laptop screen with a desktop image of the milky way. A Final-Cut-Pro file is opened, and two windows pop onto the desktop. Each shows what appears to be the same art catalogue against a yellow background. In one window, the book opens on a page with a centrefold portrait picture of native tribespeople. In the other window, the art catalogue is leafed through by a woman's carefully manicured hands. The two windows cut to superimposed clips of a young woman opening a locker in the sterile grey corridor of what seems to be an archive. These images are then paired with another window in the top right of the screen showing a Google search bar. The words "the history of the universe" are typed in the bar. What follows is a torrent of quickly-paced edited shots of Google's search images mixed with short video clips of quotidian moments, images and clips of artefacts, taxidermic flora and fauna, and a plethora of objects that form part of the vast collection of the Smithsonian Institution.

Grosse Fatigue enacts the phenomenon of the web search by overtaxing its viewers with sound and images taken from different internet sources, archival research and personal files of the artist. Different file systems and internet interfaces fill the screen—the desktop, the screensaver, folders, and windows opening and closing. These are visually linked with images of files, cabinets, boxes, and drawers in which the Smithsonian Institution preserves its collections. The rhythm and movement of the film's montage is synched to the punches of a kick-drum. A deep and warm voiceover begins to read a poem:

> *In the beginning there was no earth, no water—nothing.*
> *There was a single hill called Nunne Chaha.*
> *In the beginning everything was dead.*
> *In the beginning there was nothing, nothing at all.*
> *In the beginning there was an immense unit of energy.*
> *In the beginning there was nothing but shadow and only*
> *darkness and water and the great god of Bumba.*
> *In the beginning there were quantum fluctuations.*

> *In the beginning, the universe was a black egg where*
> *heaven and earth were mixed together.*
> *In the beginning there was an explosion.*
> *In the beginning was the eternal night Han.*
> (Henrot 2013).

The editing and drum rhythm are seamlessly synched with the spoken word poem flow, forming the backbone of *Grosse Fatigue*.

Henrot mentions in her book *Elephant Child* that the poem lines mix creation stories from various religious traditions (Hindu, Buddhist, Jewish, Christian, Islamic), hermetic traditions (kabbalah, freemasonry) and oral traditions (Dogon, Sioux, Shinto, Inuit, Navajo). In poetic recital, we hear:

> *Then the Gods split humans in two, making them each search for their lost half*
> *Then some degree of sperm competition took place*
> *Then Eve of the rib was adorned in jewellery*
> *Then a brother and sister were locked in a yellow wooden drum*
> *Then the milky way took form*
> *Then there was no need for light on Dzambu Ling,*
> *For the god emitted a pure light from their own bodies,*
> *Then the creator was in the form of a man without bones,*
> *Then the gravity of galaxies slowed the expansion of the universe,*
> *Then Ogo introduced disorder into the world by*
> *committing incest with his Mother Earth,*
> (Henrot 2013).

Henrot has a knack for image matching and juxtaposition, sound-image choreography and colour composition. Using these techniques, she forms a mesmerising dance of spoken word, drums, images, colours and movements. With this dance she attempts to tell the story of the universe's history. However, the searcher of *Grosse Fatigue* does not search for answers within the walls of the Smithsonian Institution alone. Superimposed pop-up windows open to short video clips, web texts, and web images taken from a variety of digital platforms and sources. The viewer encounters: drawers full of dead tropical birds; YouTube videos; a clip of a woman masturbating; Wikipedia lemmas; home videos; marbles; a *SkyMall* magazine; a toned male torso showering; a world map visualising occurrences of bipolar disorder; an orange rolling; a soaped naked female torso; turtles eating; a turtle hedging eggs; a frog sitting on a smartphone; flora and fauna from across cultures; as well as numerous other objects that first fill, and then flood, the screen. Henrot weaves together objects and aesthetics of oral and digital culture, natural science and theology, mixing the seemingly trivial and personal with the monumental collections of the Smithsonian Institute. Meanwhile, the spoken word poem recited in the voiceover jumbles various creation myths, moving chronologically from the beginning of creation to the end. The voiceover's tone tightens, he sounds anxious, and his breathing becomes more and more pronounced while he's heard saying:

> *The Creating Power then took many animals and birds from*
> *His great pipe bag and spread them across the earth.*
> *First came self-promoting chemicals and then fat formed membranes*
> *And then came the green algae colonies in the sea,*
> *And then the oxygen,*
> *Eight faced air, air to make winds and breezes,*
> *Air filled with sounds, air carrying oceans*
> *And then came the vertebrates, the jawless fish*
> *And then came the nautiloids in the Devonian ages of fishes,*
> *And then came amphibians from the coelacanth,*
> *And then came the birds from the coelacanth,*
> *And after the bees came the snakes,*
> *And after the snakes came the ants,*
> *And after the creodonts came the primates...*
> (Henrot 2013).

At the end, the narrator gasps for air.

Grosse Fatigue hurries through aeon and aeon. In 13 minutes, art and culture, science, extinction, Jackson Pollock, Charles Darwin, and Pantone colours are all there, as are drawings, notes, and numerous browser windows. Henrot draws no boundaries between one category and another, mashing up science, myth and the creation stories of the world; making associative leaps of imagination between objects and images of eggs, planets, marbles, a fox, and flexing biceps, spume and turtles. She synthesises disciplines and values in doing so: science and religion, words and images, epistemology and ontology. *Grosse Fatigue* seems to refuse dualisms. Who says *this* is spirituality and *that* philosophy? Who says this is *subjective* and that is *objective*?

Henrot explains in an interview: "It was my aim for the film to reflect the anxiety generated by the open nature of the world and its excessive dimension" (Henrot quoted in Picard 2013). It is the radical openness of the world that conditions anxiety. Søren Kierkegaard, one of the first theorists of anxiety, understands anxiety as a form of angst related to the limits of knowledge. Anxiety pertains to possible events that are unknown and unknowable and thus cannot be anticipated. Kierkegaard describes anxiety as an ambiguous power which both attracts and frightens us and demands that each one of us to relate to it (Kierkegaard 1844: 94-96). The question is how one relates to it, how one positions oneself in relation to it. For Kierkegaard, anxiety is both an ontological and epistemological concept. He argues that all epistemology is rooted in anxiety, and those moments of anxiety are fundamental to human existence (Kierkegaard 1844).

Frames, windows, boxes: rectangles of power-knowledge

What Google's search engine, the Smithsonian collections, and creation stories have in common are their attempts to close in on what is radically open. They attempt to organise the Great Chain of Being and the World Wide Web. Every part gets its allotted position in the whole of the natural/digital world. *Grosse Fatigue* could be seen as an enactment of the operations and mechanisms of searching as the human condition.

In the voiceover we hear:

> *And language was used to praise Heart-of-Sky rightly*
> *And humankind discovered the knowledge of history and nature*
> *Of minerals and vegetables, animals and elements*
> *The knowledge of logic and the art of thinking*
> *The sciences of gratification and those of utility,*
> *The art of remembering and pure mathematics,*
> *The science of physics, the science of medicine,*
> *The science of botany, the science of chemistry,*
> *The knowledge of politics, the knowledge of alphabets,*
> *The knowledge of magic and the science of God,*
> *The knowledge of virtue and the mechanics of poetry,*
> *The science of laws and the science of commerce,*
> *The metaphysics of bodies and the transcendental geometry,*
> *The dynamics, the hydraulics, the optics, the dioptrics,*
> *The acoustics and grammar, music, cosmology, geography,*
> *Orthography, chronology, zoology, physiology,*
> *arthology, astrology, aerology, and more.*
> *Then there was promiscuity, monogamy and polygamy...*
> (Henrot 2013).

With the pronunciation of each *logos*, a window pops up that is superimposed by the following window popping open, forming a sequence of ever-smaller rectangles within rectangles. When the narrator says "music", we are shown an image of a cassette-deck player. When he says "cosmology", we see a turtle crawling through sand. We hear "geography" and see images of a typewriter's text. "Orthography" is linked to a nest of turtle eggs in the sand. "Chronology" is linked to a picture of an analogue calculator. "Zoology" is connected to a blue bucket full of tiny turtles; "physiology" to a laptop keyboard; "pathology" to a short clip of a large number of turtles crawling over sand; "astrology" to a clip of text displayed on a light-box; 'polygamy" is linked to a clip of a chameleon being stroked by a female hand with brightly coloured polished nails.

The rhythmic popping open of windows presents a succession of images shot at the Smithsonian: corridors with file cabinets and drawers full of neatly ordered macaws, toucans, penguins, and insects are visually linked to a collection of ancient fertility statues, to X-rays of fish and seahorses. These are combined with video clips of turtles burrowing into sand, ostrich eggs being peeled, a man looking at the inside of what appears to be a nuclear bomb, a photograph of the universe, a glass eye, eyedrops falling onto a blinking eyeball, seashells, dried tree leaves, an iguana, the back of a bald head, a zebra, a boulder, pictures of bees, paintings of fish, a collection of insects, a drawer filled with taxidermized penguins, an inflatable globe, a woman sitting on the subway, and framed insects. The viewer is never informed about what kind or sort of animals, objects or rituals they are looking at, where the snippets of the footage come from or what the structure of image forms and associative ideas is supposed to convey.

Each image or clip is framed by a file window. The different fields of study and concepts listed by the narrator are visually represented as part of a larger whole made up of other disciplines that are similar to it. In *Grosse Fatigue*, all the different parts are represented by rectangles. Henrot calls these "reciprocal inclusions," and they are formally represented on screen as a stack of superimposed windows diminishing in size (Henrot 2016: 28). Like envelopes like envelopes like envelopes like. This visual play with patterns of rectangles is repeated throughout the film, like a Fibonacci sequence. In doing so, *Grosse Fatigue* stages a mesmerising audio and visual *mise en abyme* of the "different systems of belief—the different strategies used by humankind—used to synthesise human history, which is also kind of a history of the universe" (Henrot 2016: 182). That is, Henrot imagines the styles and forms of what humans consider forms of knowledge and ideas as an endless recursion of squares within squares. The search engine is yet another square within a square within another square—in an infinitely recurring sequence of squares within squares.

"Knowledge is made for cutting," Foucault once famously asserted (Foucault 1984: 88). In other words, in an attempt to understand the whole, parts are formed. In *Grosse Fatigue*, this cutting of knowledge is represented by file systems: storage boxes, file drawers, folders of computer files, and Google's search bar. These are all composed in rectangular shapes that crop, frame, and set limits. Pop-up window upon pop-up window is interspersed with footage of the neatly ordered archival facilities of the Smithsonian, suggesting a link between the different ways in which knowledge is cut out, and shaped. The rectangle signifies order that results from human intervention.

In *How to Live Together: Novelistic Simulations of Some Everyday Spaces*, Roland Barthes points to the 90- and 180-degree angles of most of the living spaces we create: houses, apartment buildings, doors, windows, roofs. "It's all rectangular ≠ nature: no rectangles... Rectangle: as the basic shape of power" (Barthes cited in Henrot, *Elephant Child*: 54). The rectangle is "the mark of the division between man and nature," Henrot claims (2016: 54). Rectangles shape the interfaces through which we navigate spaces of human dominion: databases, archives, maps, contractual papers, field guides, screens, books, and documents. Rectangles separate order from chaos. Rectangles mark off territory and separate inside from outside, what belongs, what cannot belong, and what does not fit within the four straight lines of its shape. Henrot visually emphasises the imposition of the rectangle by browser windows, folders, and files, the square vignettes and storage rooms and cabinets, boxes—the shape of order—and by juxtaposing them to spiralling objects such as shells—the shape of limitless infinitude.

The final scene of *Grosse Fatigue* shows windows opened to Wikipedia's lemma of a world map of bipolar disorder and schizophrenia and images of caged animals. Here, the maddening quest for understanding life on earth is linked to contained wilderness and psychiatric disorders with symptoms of disorganised thinking and delusion. The experience of psychiatric disorder is presented as a lemma; the "wildness" of the world is mediated through the rectangular form and straight lines of a cage. *Grosse Fatigue* associates the process of "rectangling" with the caging of animals. A pen is a closed space. Caging an animal is a safety measure. A cage reigns in the unpredictable, and tames it, domesticates it. In imposing clear boundaries, a pen makes the unpredictable, to a degree, predictable. By entering a rectangle, by putting things within a rectangle—also achieved through the preservation of objects within the rectangular spaces of an institution—a closed space is created, a space of finitude, to preserve and hold on to for eternity. Like a wild animal in a cage, the archive and the search engine contain disorder by enclosing it in a rectangle and by rendering it into an ordered list of "results" and a neat line of taxidermy animals.

The rectangle is also a key characteristic of another Google feature, the so-called Knowledge Graph. When users query a well-known person, event, place or thing, they encounter a square panel atop the search results, on mobile phone devices, or to the right of the top results, on most other devices. Google's knowledge graph feature was added to its search engine in 2012. Say one types in "Mae C. Jemison". The graph shows her full name, five portraits and headshot pictures—some older and some more recent—that are captioned "American Engineer". A short text below states,

Mae Carol Jemison is an American engineer, physician and NASA astronaut. She became the first African American woman to travel in space when she went into orbit aboard the Space Shuttle Endeavor on September 12, 1992.

Also included is an additional link to her Wikipedia lemma. In addition, it mentions her date of birth, the space mission she was on, where she went to school, awards received, and the names of her siblings. Reportedly, the information is taken from a variety of sources; however, the information provided is frequently unattributed. In October 2016, Google's C.E.O., Sundar Pichai, claimed that Google's Knowledge Graph "encompasses 70 billion facts" (Pichai quoted in Vincent 2016). That is, 70 billion search queries spawned answer boxes atop search results. Knowledge graphs also appear on contentious topics like "capital of Israel," to which Google's

Knowledge Graph answers: "Jerusalem". Query "best book of 2022" gives you a list of 42 books. Apart Chennapragada, Google's director of product management states: "So the knowledge graph is Google's understanding of the world and all the things in it" (Chennapragada quoted in Slegg 2015). This comment suggests that the world is a container of things. Its reconstruction of the world is one in which every question yields neatly ordered and boxed results. Of course, not everything can find its place in the limited coordinates of a rectangle.

Search Fever and its Discontents

The imposition of rectangles can have deadly consequences. *Grosse Fatigue* refers to ideas in Jacques Derrida's *Archive Fever: A Freudian Impression*. Derrida explores the subject of the archive from a Freudian perspective and examines the archival desire to collect and preserve in relation to what Freud called the death drive. Derrida draws attention to what remains outside of the archive, to its "forgetfulness, amnesia, the annihilation of memory" and asserts that there is "no archive without [an] outside" of that which is not preserved, or, by virtue of the archive, destroyed (Derrida 2006: 78). Henrot reflects on this paradox:

This is how the collection of endangered species ends up precipitating the complete extinction of certain species, and how some inter-categorical species cannot be named, such as certain invertebrates that are not invertebrates (Henrot 2016: 99).

No archival drive exists without a destruction drive, claims Derrida. Death haunts the Smithsonian in a literal sense. The Smithsonian's Department of Anthropology, to which Henrot had full access, was created and expanded rapidly in the context of the end of the American Indian War. As Henrot comments: "[t]he first collection contributed in an exponential way to the Smithsonian's collections was the collection of American Indian artefacts" (Henrot 2014). The Department of Anthropology has the largest collection in the world of American Indian artefacts. It illustrates Walter Benjamin's claim that "[t]here is no document of culture which is not at the same time a document of barbarism" (2003: 392).

Maintaining an ordered system always involves violence, partiality and politics. Like politics, one needs to know the rules of the game to play the game. Moreover, like a game, systems of classification contain, bound, and are rule-based. Google outsources the work of sorting, classifying, ordering, and ranking to its algorithms. This is how Google's index is formed. To be part of its index, rules are established. Rules not only point to what is allowed and what not—to what is indexed and what not—but also to who sets the rules and who owns the index. An index, as is well known, is a tool of arrangement. Google's index is a means to create a system of order in what would otherwise be perceived as a chaotic multitude. To index is to practice exclusions. Exclusions generate a list of results with a top and bottom. There can be no index or ranked results without cutting, discarding, and excluding. An index makes available and unavailable, connects and disconnects, and interconnects, recognises, misrecognises, and unrecognises. Therefore, what is considered part of its index is subjective, contingent, and self-referential.

Further, the unknown is rendered as both an ontological and epistemological problem. Not knowing the whole story, not being able "to make sense" out of a vast and chaotic multitude, is associated with losing one's mind—in the form of images of a Wikipedia lemma about schizophrenia and bipolar disorder—and with death. *Grosse Fatigue*'s point is that some things cannot be detached from subjectivity. Queries into Google's vast database or the Smithsonian's collection are mediated and governed queries within the bounded space of the web and the archive, which are limited spaces and bounded by time. By overestimating what Google, the Smithsonian and creation stories can provide, *Grosse Fatigue*'s searcher is seized by anxiety. Questions regarding existence cannot be answered by data or documents alone. Further, many things in human existence cannot be documented, transfixed, factually accounted for, indexed or datafied, or reduced to facts. Queries may have 'hits' and 'results' but no conclusive *answers*.

"We will wander, improvise, fall short and move in circles" (Halberstam 2011: 25). Henrot frames web search anxiety as the relation between, on the one hand, the radical openness of knowledge and actuality; *and*, on the other hand, the rigid algorithmic regimes that circumscribe this openness self-referentially.

Searchers as Collectors of Stories

Collections depend on systems of ordering. In the essay "Unpacking my Library", Walter Benjamin writes: "[t]here is in the life of a collector a dialectical tension between the poles of disorder and order" (1999: 60). Another dialectical tension he points to in *The Arcades Project* is between the collector and the allegorist, when he writes: "in every collector hides an allegorist, and in every allegorist a collector" (Benjamin 2002: 211).

In *Grosse Fatigue,* the dialectical play between order and disorder and between the collector and allegorist resembles a Google search engine at high-speed. The loose associations between words and images are immediately followed by other image associations or juxtapositions that, in turn, are supported by other quick associative links between images, between image and spoken word, and within images. Further, the editing of *Grosse Fatigue* resembles a synthesis of order and disorder. Images of spiralling objects reoccur in *Grosse Fatigue*. As is well known, the spiral is the structure of the infinite, the unlimited and the endless—it represents chaos. Henrot represents order by way of desktop folders, browser windows, archival storage facilities and other ordering systems. These are interspersed with clips and images taken at the Smithsonian of lockers being opened or closed and panned images of its endless corridors filled with file cabinets and boxes. These rectangles and practices of order find their spiral counterparts in the next scene. A small file window hovers over others at the centre of the desktop screen. In this window, we see a video of a laptop playing a film. The film shows a man stumbling down a tungsten-lit institutional hallway. He falls against one wall, then against the other, trying to maintain some balance to quickly topple and fall to the ground. The film is a clip from Rainer Werner Fassbinder's *World on a Wire* (1973), a German science fiction T.V. series showing the possibility that the world exists entirely inside another world. Fred Stiller, the series' protagonist, struggles to keep his sanity in this web of worlds within worlds in which the lines between simulation, representation and the real are blurred. *Grosse Fatigue* suggests that when searching for answers about the history of the cosmos, we are all Fred Stiller, thereby linking search engine anxiety to the limits of knowledge. The whole escapes our grasp. Henrot writes,

The museum [Smithsonian Natural History Museum] is like a neurosis… Everything must enter the museum: everything living, dying, or deceiving; all the fish in the sea, all the birds in the sky, all the animals of the forest. The aim of the Smithsonian's Natural History Museum—to be a museum of everything—is an irrational project that is driven by the wish, the ambition, to reconstitute a world (Henrot 2016: 80).

Grosse Fatigue enacts web search as a form of collecting *within* a collection. This reframes our searching condition and the act that gives form to it, collecting. As Henrot performs it in *Grosse Fatigue*, collecting does not signal a break from, nor exceed, the bounded and finite spaces of Google's indexed web. Indeed, to search is to collect *within* Google's collection. *Grosse Fatigue* results from Henrot's collection of a collection curated by people at the Smithsonian Institution and by Google's algorithms. What is the function of the collection for Henrot? Where does this imaginary take us? A collector gathers fragments from a world outside of their control to rebuild a world within their confines and control. According to Benjamin the collector arranges a miniature of the universe—a globe within a globe (Benjamin 2002: 208). The collector's "deepest desire" is to "renew the old world," Benjamin writes (Benjamin 1999: 61). To collect is to re-create a world cleansed of frustration, like a miniature world—"a box in the theatre of the world" (Benjamin 2002: 19).

Collections make connections; they have a fictional quality; they tell a story. Forming a collection could be considered as the construction of a story. To collect is to re-create a story within a story. The Smithsonian collection, it could be argued, is a creation story in reverse order. It attempts to make a whole out of fragments. By contrast, the list of URL results Google's search engine offers moves from link to link and makes connections that could be seen as selecting fragments from the whole. Forming a collection could be considered as the construction of a story in a box in the theatre of the world, as Benjamin describes it. The box, the collection, may represent a story, value or an idea around which a collector frames their activities; not outside of or separate from, but within the world.

What does narrativisation offer? A narrative provides linear structure, a before and an after, and causation within a limited space. Creation stories are linear stories of classification. They are often represented as following a linear, progressive structure that clusters and organises events around a continuum—*and then came the vertebrates, the jawless fish. And then came the nautiloids in the Devonian ages of fishes.* Stories also offer a sense of location and direction. This is how it began, we are *here* now, and *this* is how it ends—*and on the Seventh Day...* Like a narrative, science organises its forms and contents into a series of events and gives them meaning. Every collection creates a story, re-tells a creation story, and collects stories within stories. By arranging objects, a collector produces a narrative. The reappearance of hands that click, double-click, reject and select in *Grosse Fatigue* emphasise the ability to "edit" a story or a play, as well as the ability to become a creator of those stories. Different stories can be told by making different selections or using the same objects but ordering them differently. A collection forms part of an infinite spiral of possible stories in a finite and bounded space. Searching-as-collecting and the searcher-as-collector offer a relational play with components and connections between fact and fiction, and the finite and the infinite, order and disorder. *Grosse Fatigue* represents a web search as an activity filled with contradictions. It enacts web search as the result of a continuous exchange between two opposites that influence each other: the analogue and the digital, the historical and the contemporary, the factual and the fictional, faith and reason.

Quests for knowledge are about thinking *and* being. Kierkegaard writes, "thinking and being signify one and the same" (Kierkegaard 1846: 407). Kierkegaard would insist that these narrative spaces of collectors are not autarchic spaces; they are never cleansed of frustration nor rinsed clear of uncertainties. They remain self-referential. Search queries are constantly haunted by the limits of knowledge, by dispersion, by disorder, which stains the neat list of results offered to the searcher. The collector, in the end, chases its own tail. At the same time, to reframe searching as collecting within a collection is a limited and time-sensitive gesture oriented toward different narrations, relations, and cohabitations inside and outside Google's engine.

What remains is the inherent uncertainty, subjectivity and self-referentiality of human knowledge, the inaccessibility of earthlings to a view from nowhere— to objective knowledge. This is expressed in *Grosse Fatigue* by emphasising the loneliness of the Gods in creation stories. While we hear heavy breathing, the voiceover of Grosse Fatigue continues to tell in mournful tone what happened on the Seventh day:

And Bumba vomited up the sun, and the sun dried
up some water, leaving land
Woman Who Fell From the Sky rested on turtle's back

> *God blessed the seventh day and sanctioned it,*
> *Because that in it He had rested from all his work.*
> *The arrow of time points to the heath death of the universe.*
> *And Pan Gu felt lonely*
> *And Heart-of-Sky felt lonely with the loneliness that ends the worlds.*
> *Who can understand the loneliness of Gods?*
> *Yaweh was lonely*
> *And Ogo was lonely*
> *Lonely like Wak and lonely like Allah.*
> *The whole earth was heavy and then Yahweh rested.*
> *...resting, Pan Gu laid down*
> *and resting, he died*
> (Henrot 2013).

Seen this way, searching as collecting and collecting as storytelling is a way to move in and out of a world without permanent certainties or rather, with only one permanent certainty.

References

Becker, Konrad /Stadler, Felix (2010): Deep search: The politics of search beyond Google, Vienna: Studien Verlag.
Benjamin, Walther (1999): "Unpacking my library." In: Hannah Arendt (ed.), Illuminations, London: Pimlico.
Benjamin, Walther (2002): The Arcades project. (Howard, E./McLaughlin, K. Trans.), Cambridge: Harvard University Press.
Benjamin, Walther (2003): "On the concept of history." In: Walther Benjamin, Selected Writings: Volume 4, 1938-1940, Cambridge: The Belknap Press of Harvard University Press.
Bucher, Taina (2018): If...Then: Algorithmic power and politics, Oxford: Oxford University Press.
Campanelli, Vito (2014): "Frictionless sharing: The rise of automatic criticism." In: René König/Miriam Rasch (eds.), Society of the query reader: reflections on web search, Amsterdam: Institute of Network Cultures.
Chun, Wendy Hui Kyong (2006): Control and freedom. Power and paranoia in the age of fiber optics, Cambridge, MA: The MIT Press.
Couldry, Nick (2012): Media, society, world: Social theory and digital media practice, Cambridge: Polity Press.
Derrida, Jacques (2006): "Archive fever." In: Charles Merewether (ed.), The archive: Documents of contemporary art, London: Whitechapel.

Dourish, Paul (2016): "Algorithms and their others: Algorithmic culture in context." Big Data & Society 3/2. https://doi.org/10.1177/2053951716665128

Dutton, W. H./Reisdorf, B./Dubois, E./Blank, G. (2017): "Search and politics: The uses and impacts of search in Britain, France, Germany, Italy, Poland, Spain, and the United States." SSRN. Retrieved from: http://dx.doi.org/10.2139/ssrn.2960697

Epstein, Robert (2019, July 15): "To break Google's monopoly on search, make its index public." Bloomberg Businessweek. Retrieved from https://www.bloomberg.com/news/articles/2019-07-15/to-break-google-s-monopoly-on-search-make-its-index-public

Epstein, Robert/Robertson, Ronald E. (2015): "The search engine manipulation effect (SEME) and its possible impact on the outcomes of elections." PNAS, 112/33. Retrieved from https://doi.org/10.1073/pnas.1419828112

Foucault, Michel (1984): "Nietzsche, genealogy, history." In: Paul Rabinow (ed.), The Foucault Reader, New York: Pantheon.

Fuchs, Christian (2012): "Google capitalism." TripleC - Cognition, Communication, Co-operation, 10/1, pp. 42-48.

Galloway, Alexander R. (2006): Gaming: Essays on algorithmic culture, Minnesota: Minnesota University Press.

Gehl, Robert W. (2014): Reverse engineering Social Media: Software, culture, and political economy in new media capitalism, Philadelphia: Temple University Press.

Google Search (2019): "How search works: Our mission." Retrieved from https://www.google.com/search/howsearchworks/mission/

Halberstam, Judith (2011): The queer art of failure, Durham and London: Duke University Press.

Halpern, Orit (2014): Beautiful data. A history of vision and reason since 1945, London: Duke Press.

Henrot, Camille (2016). "Elephant Child." In: Camille Henrot/Clara Meister/Michael Connor/Kristina Scepanski/Monique Jeudy-Ballini (eds.), Camille Henrot: Elephant Child, New York, NY: Inventory Press & London: Koenig Books.

Hoffmann, Anna Lauren (2019): "Where fairness fails: data, algorithms, and the limits of antidiscrimination discourse." Information, Communication & Society, 22/7, 900-915. https://doi.org/10.1080/1369118X.2019.1573912

Jarrett, Kylie (2014): "A database of intention." In: René König/Miriam Rasch (eds.), Society of the query reader: reflections on web search, Amsterdam: Institute of Network Cultures.

Jiang, Min (2013): "The business and politics of search engines: A comparative study of Baidu's and Google's search results of Internet events in China." New Media & Society, 16/2. https://doi.org/10.1177/1461444813481196

Jobin, Anna/Glassey, Olivier (2014): "'I am not a web search result! I am a free word': The categorization and commodification of 'Switzerland' by Google."

In: René König/Miriam Rasch (eds.), Society of the query reader: reflections on web search, Amsterdam: Institute of Network Cultures.

Jordan, Tim (2015): Information politics: Liberation and exploitation in the digital society, London: Pluto Press.

Kierkegaard, Soren ([1844] 2014): The concept of anxiety. A simple psychologically oriented deliberation in view of the dogmatic problem of hereditary Sin (A. Hannay, Trans. & Ed.), New York, NY: Liveright Publishing Company.

Kierkegaard, Soren ([1846] 1992): Concluding unscientific postscript to philosophical fragments, Volume 1 (Hong H.V. & Hong, E.H., Trans & Eds.), Princeton, NJ: Princeton University Press.

Knight, Simon/Mercer, Neil (2015): "The role of exploratory talk in classroom search engine tasks." Technology, Pedagogy and Education, 24/3, pp. 309-319. https://doi.org/10.1080/1475939X.2014.931884

Kolbert, Elisabeth (2017, August 21): "Who owns the Internet?" The New Yorker. Retrieved from https://www.newyorker.com/magazine/2017/08/28/who-owns-the-internet

Lewandowski, Dirk (2014): "Why We Need an Independent Index of the Web". In: René König/Miriam Rasch (eds.), Society of the query reader: reflections on web search, Amsterdam: Institute of Network Cultures.

Mager, Astrid (2012): "Algorithmic ideology: How capitalist society shapes search engines." Information, Communication & Society, 15/5, pp. 769-787.

Noble, Safiya Omoja (2018): Algorithms of oppression, New York, NY: New York University Press.

Ørmen, Jacob (2014): "Historicizing Google search: A discussion of the challenges related to archiving search results." In: René König/Miriam Rasch (eds.), Society of the query reader: reflections on web search, Amsterdam: Institute of Network Cultures.

Ørmen, Jacob (2016): "Googling the news: Opportunities and challenges in studying news events through Google search." Digital Journalism, 4/1. https://doi.org/10.1080/21670811.2015.1093272

Pariser, Eli (2011): The Filter Bubble: How the new personalized web is changing what we read and how we think, London: Penguin Books.

Petzold, Thomas (2011): "The Merkel algorithm. What Indian search engines reveal about German chancellor Angela Merkel?" Zeitschrift fuer internationale Perspektiven, 2-3, pp. 76.

Picard, Andrea (2013): "Camille Henrot: A hunter-gatherer during a time of collective 'Grosse Fatigue'." Cinema Scope, CS56. Retrieved from http://cinema-scope.com/columns/tiff-2013-preview-grosse-fatigue-camille-henrot-france usa/

Slegg, Jennifer (2015, May 29): "Google has over 1 billion knowledge graph entities in search results." The Sem Post. Retrieved from http://www.thesempost.com/google-1-billion-knowledge-graph-search-results/

Smithsonian Institution (n.d.): "Smithsonian purpose and vision." Retrieved from https://www.si.edu/about/mission

Striphas, Ted (2015): "Algorithmic culture." European Journal of Cultural Studies, 18/4-5, pp. 395-412.

Vaidhyanathan, Siva (2011): The googlization of everything: (and why we should worry), Oakland, CA: University of California Press.

Vincent, James (2016, October 4): "Apple boasts about sales; Google boasts about how good its AI is." The Verge, Retrieved from https://www.theverge.com/2016/10/4/13122406/google-phone-event-stats

Art Works Cited

Groten, Anja (2013): Machina Recordatio [sound installation], Public Library of Amsterdam, Society of the Query Conference, Amsterdam, 2013.

Henrot, Camille (2013): Grosse Fatigue [video, 13 min], GLOBALE: Exo-Evolution, ZKM, Karlsruhe, 2015.

Holmes, Harlo/Henrot, Camille (2015): Desktopmance [application].

Jones, Phil/Amir, Aharon (2009): Narcissus Search Engine for N.E.W.S. [web application] Retrieved from http://searchnarcissus.net/

Simon, Taryn (2012): Image Atlas. Retrieved from http://www.imageatlas.org/

Cybernetics and the early experiments in Computer Art

Angela Krewani

Abstract

The current debate on artificial intelligence (AI) has been shaped by the fascination for the complex abilities and conceptual range of AI on the one hand, on the other hand, this debate voices the fear of losing artistic autonomy and the creative human subject. These discourses on artistic autonomy are still important, especially for the contemporary art system, which still requires the individual artist to be the outstanding creator. This idea is still relevant for the contemporary art market, even if there are large revenues with algorithmic art (cp. Scorzin 2021).
This essay looks into the history of digital media and digital art and concentrates on concepts that embrace the connection between art and algorithm as creative and innovative. The European debate of the 1950s and 1960s which revolved around such terms as "cybernetics", "informational aesthetics" or "computer art" cheered the technical abilities of the computer and reflected upon the new aesthetic potential. In the following I want to concentrate on the history of artificial intelligence and digital art, where the relationship between computers and creativity was not understood as a threat to artistic and aesthetic values, but as aesthetic innovation. This historic understanding of computers as artistic creators uncovers a forgotten path into contemporary digital art and AI-art.

Keywords

cybernetics, computer art, creativity, cultural practices in the US and Germany

Cybernetics as conceptual background for digital creativity

Within the genealogy of computer art, cybernetic theory plays an important role, since it provides the background for aesthetic concepts of loops and feedback structures, as it is demonstrated in the works e.g. of Gordon Pask, which will be discussed later. Regardless of technological innovations, cybernetics was prominent in the 1940s and 1950s, accordingly, it developed in conjunction with computer technologies, but it expressed a theory which was concerned with interacting systems and feedback structures, which provided a base for AI and its respective art forms.

As a scientific theory of automatism, organization and calculating machines, cybernetics developed between the 1930s and 1950s as an interdisciplinary project between natural and technological sciences, arts and humanities. Cybernetics sought to suspend the gap between natural sciences and humanities to establish a joint scientific culture that could explain social organizations, organisms and technological structures with the same methodological tools. Thus it claimed dominance in all realms of human life, starting with religion and ending with art and psychiatry (Müller 2008: 7). This wide conceptual radius allowed for the transference of cybernetic concepts into artistic production since the aspect of technology was pushed to the margins as was the question of individual artistic authorship. Cybernetics focused on the dynamics of systems, the individual artist was no part of it.

Although cybernetics has failed to fulfill its claim as an all-encompassing scientific approach, it has influenced manifold discourses on literature, art and media, and it reaches into the current discussion on media and general ecologies (Hörl 2016). Chiefly Norbert Wiener's positions underline the creative aspects of cybernetic art in two regards: It is the idea of sensors as an extension of human senses in the context of the cybernetic equation of organic and technological beings. These conflations are partly realized in contemporary AI Art when we consider networks with human and non-human agents (Scorzin 2021: 48). The second aspect hints at contemporary societies. Following Wiener, these can be exclusively understood through the study of its communication channels, which presuppose the communication between humans and machines.

Cybernetics offers the conceptual basis for contemporary art forms such as interactive-, performance and digital art since it applies models of information and communication. Katherine Hayles offers a three-stage model of aesthetic practices, which she labels as

1. homeostasis: feedback loops, circular causality, instrumental language;
2. reflexivity: reflexive language, autopoiesis, structural coupling;
3. virtuality: emergent behaviour, functionality, computer universe. (Hayles 1999: 40ff)

These categories are not understood as succeeding models, they better describe the range of approaches to aesthetic production. These models turn away from notions such as aesthetic value, representation or archive; they instead foster a systemic dynamics of artistic creation regardless of their technological state. It could be requested how far they imply a technological structure. They function as the discursive environment of technological concepts and in this realm, the distance between well-defined technology and a more abstract concept is part of the aesthetics of technology, as Gilbert Simondon lets us know:

The real perfecting of machines, which we can say raises the level of technicality, does not correspond to an increase in automatism but, on the contrary, relates to the fact that the functioning of the machine conceals a certain margin in indetermination. It is such a margin that allows for the machine's sensitivity to outside information. It is this sensitivity to information on part of machines, much more than any increase in automatism that makes possible a technical ensemble. A purely automatic machine completely closed in on itself in a predetermined operation could only give summary results. (Simondon 1980 [1958]: 4)

Following Katherine Hayles' categories and Simondon's remarks on the margins of technology, the relationship between technology and art can produce aesthetic structures.

Although the technological environment of cybernetics was – compared to current digital technologies – less-developed, cybernetics offered reflections on the aesthetics of interacting systems. Fascinated by the systemic operations of feedback systems, artists and theoreticians offered aesthetic projects and fantasies, which later on would be standardized through innovative technologies. Although art and aesthetic production had not been a central interest of cybernetic theory, its environment proved fruitful for creative art projects. Interestingly enough, cybernetics brought about a variety of artistic experiments, which conflated cybernetic theory with experiments in computer graphics. One of the leading exhibitions had been *Electronic Abstractions* (Cherokee, IOWA, 1953), which figures as the first exhibition of "computer art". It was conceptualized as a touring exhibition and it presented 50 photos of Ben J. Lapowsky's series "Oscillons". The images had been produced with a computer, realized on a cathode-ray-oscillograph and photographed from the screen (Piehler 2002: 45).

The first European exhibition was presented in London in 1968 with the title *Cybernetic Serendipity,* being curated by Jasia Reichardt, whom it took three years to organize the exhibition. Facing the rising presence of computers in the military and the administration, Reichardt looked out for their potential in the creative world. Computers, she stated, "have so far neither revolutionized music, nor art, nor poetry, in the same way, they have revolutionized science" (McCray 2022: 696). For this reason, she decided

to showcase the 'possibilities' of computers and other 'cybernetic devices' as well as the 'relationships between technology and creativity'. She wanted to demonstrate the often-unseen linkages between computers, cybernetics, and creativity, with examples of 'machine-aided' creative processes. (ibid: 696)

As has been characteristic of the early computer- and media art, Reichardt discovered her exhibits in cooperation with the young computer industry and research institutes of technology (Piehler 2002: 51). Regardless of the art works' origins, this was the first world exhibition of what later on was called "media art", since it covered experiments with light, graphics and animation, kinetic objects and interactive installations.

The press release for the London shows underlines the exhibition's technological features and its proximity to cybernetics.

Cybernetics—derives from the Greek "kybernetes" meaning steersman; our word governor comes from the Latin version of the same word. The term cybernetics was first used by Norbert Wiener around 1948. In 1948 his book "Cybernetics" was subtitled "Communication and Control in Animal and Machine". The term today refers to systems of communication and control in complex electronic devices like computers, which have very definite similarities with the processes of communication and control in the human nervous system. A cybernetic device responds to stimulus from outside and in turn affects the external environment, like a thermostat which responds to the coldness of a room by switching on the heating and thereby altering the temperature. This process is called feedback. Exhibits in the show are either produced with a cybernetic device (computer) or are cybernetic devices in themselves. They react to something in the environment, either human or machine, and in response produce either sound, light or movement. Serendipity – was coined by Horace Walpole in 1754. There was a legend about three princes of Serendip (old name for Ceylon) who used to travel throughout the world and whatever was their aim or whatever they looked for, they always found something very much better. Walpole used the term serendipity to describe the faculty of making happy chance discoveries. Through the use of cybernetic devices to make graphics, film and poems, as well as other randomizing machines which interact with the spectator, many happy discoveries were made. Hence the title of this show.

Also striking is the optimistic attitude towards the technological challenge: technology was to be considered as innovation within the artistic experience, as art historian David Mellon has affirmed concerning cybernetic art.

A dream of technical control and instant information conveyed at unthought-of velocities haunted Sixties culture. The wired, electronic outlines of a cybernetic society became apparent to the visual imagination of an immediate future [....] drastically modernized by the impact of computer science. It was a technologically utopian structure of feeling, positivistic and 'scientistic'. (Mellor in Sahnken 2001: x)

One of the famous presenters of this show was the British artist and theorist Gordon Pask (Fernández 2008, 163). A perfect example of cybernetic art without technology is the works of the British cybernetician Gordon Pask, being born in Derby, England in 1928 and died in London in 1996. Gordon Pask developed his artistic ideas from his cybernetic research, followingly he figures as one of the most prominent and least known English cyberneticians (Fernández 2008: 163). As Pickering affirms, Pask's involvement in cybernetics started in the theatre, where he participated as an undergraduate and together with Robin McKinnon-Wood founded a theatre company called "Sirenelle", which was dedicated to staging musical comedies (Pickering 2002: 426). Gordon Pask expressed interest in the integration of a computer into the theatre-performances and constructed a "succession of odd and interesting machines, running from a Musical Typewriter, through a self-adapting metronome to the so-called 'Musicolour machine'" (ibid.). The Musicolour machine was a cybernetic device that functioned like a homeostat, a performance

centred on a feedback loop running from the human performer through the musical instrument and the machine itself into the environment (light show), and thence back to the performer. (ibid.: 427)

Pickering goes on and argues that the human part of the machine could interact with the machine and explore the infinite possibilities offered in this contact (ibid.).

Pask's oeuvre consists of 6 books on education and cybernetics, 200 essays, music and plays as well as artistic projects (Fernández 2008: 163). His best-known work, the *Colloquy of Mobiles*, being presented at the exhibition in London, was developed out of his interest in communication and communicative feedback loops. Contrary to some of the neighbouring artworks, the *Colloquy* did not directly interact with a computer: Pask arranged five large mobiles hanging from a metal bar at the ceiling, interacting with each other. The mobiles were "tri-dimensional sculptures powered by motors, individually programmed and also partly computer-driven". The computer was experimentally developed, and it was hidden in the metal bar at the ceiling (ibid.: 165). The single elements were provided with a goal that permitted interaction and communication. In terms of the self-organization of systems, Fernández offers the following conclusion.

Colloquy met some of the requirements for self-organizing systems that Pask had identified 10 years earlier. In his opinion, self-organizing systems were systems that we regard as though they have elements in them that make decisions. (Fernández 2008: 166)

The Cultural Dimensions of Cybernetics

The euphoric attitude towards cybernetics' possibilities is also voiced in the social and cultural discourses of the 1960s and 1970s, as the Expo 1967 in Toronto demonstrated, which focused on cybernetics in all aspects of cultural and social life (Borck 2008). Even the idea of the Planet Earth and its ecologies, which has currently been prominent, was based on the connection between early cybernetics, computer- and counterculture, as Fred Turner demonstrates (Turner 2008: 69–102).

During the 1960s, cybernetics seemed to offer an all-encompassing social utopia. Consequently, in his essay "Cybernetics and Human Culture", Marshall McLuhan praised cybernetics as the basis for a new understanding of contemporary societies.

If we speak in configurational terms, cybernation tends to restore the integral and inclusive patterns of work and learning that had characterized the age of the hunter and the food-gatherer but tended to fade with the rise of the Neolithic or specialist revolution in human work and activity. Paradoxically, the electronic age of cybernation is unifying and integrating, whereas the mechanical age had been fragmenting and dissociating [....] Another way of looking at our situation today in the age of cybernation and information machines is to say that from the time of origin of script and wheel, men have been engaged in extending their bodies technologically. They have created instruments that simulated and exaggerated and fragmented our various physical powers for the exertion of force [...] Electricity made possible the extension of the human nervous system as a new social environment [...] The artist tends to be a man who is fully aware of the environmental. (McLuhan 2003: 47–49)

With these remarks, McLuhan formulates some of the dominant topics within the discussion on digital art and artificial intelligence, which relate to the network structure of digital communication and the much-discussed topic of electricity as an extension of the nervous system, which is played through in literature, film and digital art.

Besides these theoretical positions, cybernetics infused media theory such as Michael Shamberg's *Guerilla Television* (Shamberg 1971) and Gene Youngblood's *Expanded Cinema* (Youngblood 1970). Michael Shamberg's publication discursively conflates cybernetics and countercultures to raise a critical consciousness for a media revolution, which revolves around the television. His journal *Radical Software* offers a mixture of cybernetic theory, media- and television criticism. Similarly, Gene Youngblood's *Expanded Cinema* marks the typical conflation of cybernetic theory with utopian thinking. Imitating the discourse of underground writing, he considers cybernetic as the underlying power for the media change from analogue to electronic communication media.

We're in transition from the Industrial Age to the Cybernetic Age, characterized by many as the Post-Industrial Age. But I've found the term *Paleocybernetic* valuable as a conceptual tool with which to grasp the significance of our present environment: combining the primitive potential associated with the Paleolithic and the transcendental integrities of 'practical utopianism' associated with Cybernetic. I call it the Paleocybernetic Age: an image of a hairy, buckskinned, barefooted atomic physicist with a brain full of mescaline and logarithms, working out the heuristics of computer-generated holograms or krypton laser interferometry. It's the dawn of man: for the first time in history, we'll soon be free enough to discover who we are. (Youngblood 1970: 350)

In the chapter on "Cybernetic Cinema and Computer Films", Youngblood concentrates on the experiments with digital film, in which he considers the computer as an agent within aesthetic production, hence uncoupling the computer from the administrative-military complex and contextualizing him within artistic production (Youngblood 1970: 256).

Fig. 1: Cover of Radical Software, Number 2 (1970), a print magazine that detailed emerging trends in video, television, and early computing.

For Youngblood, digital visuality is brought about by the aesthetic processes, which are generated by the computer, he quotes Jack Burnham's early attempt at defining technological art in his essay on "System Esthetics".

Scientists and technicians are not converted into artists, rather the artist becomes a symptom of the schism between art and technics. Progressively, the need to make ultrasensitive judgements as to the uses of technology and scientific information becomes 'art' in the most literal sense. (Burnham qt. in Youngblood 1970: 207)

Referring to the curator, artist and art historian Jack Burnham, Gene Youngblood mentions the leading intellectuals in the realm of cybernetics and art. Understanding how deeply cybernetics was entangled in the military complex, he tried to redefine it in the context of contemporary art. He saw the art world in transition "from an *object-oriented* to *system-oriented culture*" (McCray 2022: 699). The quote above also voices his conviction that technology and system-oriented thinking would become part of aesthetic creation, thus one of his main intentions was "applying systems theory to contemporary art" (ibid.).

Fig. 2: Guerilla television, a guide to breaking through the barriers of mainstream television. Shamberg and Raindance Corporation. New York: Holt, Rinehart and Winston, 1973.

Burnham himself is also well connected with technology research within the academic context; in 1968 he spent one year with research at MIT's newly established Center for Advanced Visual Studies (CAVS) and sought tutorials with among others Marvin Minksy and C.R. Licklider (ibid.). In 1970, after his fellowship at MIT, Burnham organized an exhibition with the title *Software. Information Technology: It's Meaning for Arts* "to take place at the Jewish Museum in Manhattan.

The exhibition is planned to bring about collaborations between artists and technicians" (ibid.: 690). Although the exhibition was not successful, it demonstrated the artistic and social dimension of cybernetics and the approach to new, digital technologies.

In the US-American culture and society, cybernetics was very present during the 1960s and 1970s, since it experienced its separation from the military complex and its integration into the cultural discourses. It thus carried references within the countercultural discourses and it impacted the art world and its aesthetic processes. Not just in the realm of computer technology and simulation, but also concepts such as feedback processes and interactivity had been explored. The media of these explorations had not been restricted to the computer, but these processes had been widely explored within the medium video and its inherent feedback structures, as the works of Les Levine or Woody and Steina Vasulka demonstrate (Krewani 2016: 123–30).

Cybernetics as artistic technology

In contrast to the USA, the connection between art and cybernetics described a different development, as it was determined by the technical universities on the one hand, but enjoyed less popularity on the other, as Fred Turner argues (Turner 2008). The German intention was mainly to continue cybernetic art as aesthetic practice; accordingly, the interactive, communicative aspects of this theory were pushed aside. This development may have been due to the engagement of the philosopher Max Bense, who taught philosophy and scientific theory at the Technical University in Stuttgart and who was one of the main proponents of cybernetic theory. This background differs immensely from the US-American cybernetic community that was part of an underground culture or an artistic crowd. Bense's interests in aesthetic processes kept up concepts of 'art' and 'aesthetics', and it strongly opposed the avant-garde theory of Fluxus- and Happening art, which became prominent in the 1960s.

Following the theoretical work of the mathematician George D. Birkhoff, who had developed a formula for aesthetic order and complexity. Max Bense introduced a theoretical approach to aesthetic processes and inherent complexities, in his thinking, art functions as a "generator for innovation", aesthetics equals technologies, and it can compete with the natural sciences (Hörl/Hagner 2008: 35). Bense's concept does not refer to the practical aspects of computer technologies, and neither does he conceptualize digital cultures. His concept of density of information (Informationsdichte) turns into an aesthetic theory.

It is [...] easy to see that the measure of creation as the measure of innovation is given by the contribution of information, while the measure of communication as the measure of order is sensibly determined by the contribution of redundancy. Any measure of creation further achieves what is expressed by the classical art-theoretical term originality, while the measure in which an aesthetic state or a work of art becomes communicable or can be identified is a question of its recognisable order, as a redundancy, which roughly corresponds to the classical term of style. (Bense 1998: 316, translation Angela Krewani)

With the impact of the informational density as an aesthetic and creative concept Bense offers a theory of art that overrides the limits of computer art, he states a change in the aesthetic consciousness. In Bense's context technology functions as a superior instance to bypass contradictions. Art is not evaluated along the lines of historical categories but along the lines of technological standards which stand for objectivity and functionality. Here Bense concludes:

With the transition from historical to technical consciousness, a new relationship to time is obviously expressed. Apart from the fact that the classical concept of education is essentially oriented towards the historical past and is increasingly being replaced by a new one whose meaning and level are determined by the future of our civilisation and its technical reality, future history, i.e. the temporality that lies openly before us, proves to be the essential, the decisive one within technical consciousness. (Bense 1956: 16)

Bense's concepts keep up the ideas of 'aesthetics' and 'art', but they displace them into technological discourses. Technology hovers as the key concept. Unfortunately, these ideas are not central to German avant-garde art with the cultures of happenings and Fluxus as well as the prominence of the artist Joseph Beuys, who refuted ideas of technology and art. Claus Pias contrasts the avantgarde-movement with Bense's somehow elaborated concept of art and concludes that around 1970 the case of Bense's cybernetics was lost. The 1968 students' movement and the prevalence of spontaneous models of art had finished off Bense's sometimes peculiar technicality (Pias 2008: 79).

Following Pias's estimation and comparing the German and the US-American situation we can observe a difference. Cybernetics within the American culture could develop as a cultural and pop-cultural factor. As has already been argued in this essay, cybernetics connected to underground- and countercultures, transferred into the early computer industry (Turner 2008: 103–40) and disseminated into a variety of art forms, which were not directly connected to the computer, e.g. the experiments of early video-culture and the closed-circuit-installations (Krewani 2016: 123–30). Additionally, based on cybernetics, artists like Roy Ascott developed concepts of digital networking long before the technical realization could happen. His famous essay on "Behaviourist Art and the Cybernetic Vision" features the communicative, practical dimensions of cybernetics. Art in this context emerges from the interaction of "variety and irritation" (Ascott 2003: 147) but contrary to Max Bense, Ascott's vision addressed forms of communicative art, which could only be realized in a democratic communication society.

Instant communication, the simultaneity of events, multidirectional references and associations, incessant stimulation of all the senses, and the active participation of each human being are factors that constitute an energetic core of creative activity. "Only a fully automated society, or a society in process of being shaped by a cybernetic vision, would require this degree of artificially supported creative intensity, and only the cybernetic era could be expected to maintain it." (Ascott 2003: 147) "We are moving towards a fully cybernated society [...] where processes of retroaction, instant communication, and autonomic flexibility will inform every aspect of our environment." (ibid.: 126)

Ascott's thinking as well as the other factors promoted the connection between aesthetic communication and artistic practices. Hence the US-American approaches had been able to integrate spontaneous and underground artistic practices, contrary to the German situation, where the gap between art forms remained open. This may also have been due to the diehard German mistrust of technology and mass media, which was a consequence of Nazi media politics.

This isolation between social movements and artistic practices could also be found in the experiments around computer graphics, which emerged at technical universities in Germany, which is attributed to the general term "computer art" and focusing exclusively on the computer as an artistic tool. The first exhibitions took place in 1969 at the "Studiengalerie der Technischen Hochschule" and the "Galerie Niedlich", both located in Stuttgart. The German Goethe Institute supported these exhibitions and organized an international touring exhibition with the title "Impuls Computerkunst". Contrary to the British *Cybernetic Serendipity* it focused exclusively on the computer (Piehler 2002: 12–25). The theoretical basis for the artistic experiments with the computer had been developed by Helmar Frank, a member of the circle around Bense and at that time principal of the Pädagogische Hochschule Berlin. Interestingly enough, Frank refrained from the term "art" in favour of the terms "aesthetic information" and "aesthetic objects", regarding the lack of consciousness within the computer as a main argument against the term "art". He states that

however, works of art produced by an automaton are [...] not works of art, because we are—at least still today—incapable of attributing a consciousness to their source, the automaton. (Frank in Piehler 2002: 196)

This interesting argument, which seems to be so prevalent in the German discussion on digital art, is still to be found today in the context of artificial intelligence or algorithmic art.

Also cognizant of Bense's aesthetic theories, Herbert W. Franke applied his ideas in his computer experiments, which he termed "informational aesthetics" (Informationsästhetik). His 1974 publication *Die kybernetischen Grundlagen der Ästhetik (The cybernetic basis of aesthetics)* locates the cybernetic approach already in its title. Although not considering cybernetics as an aesthetic theory, he states its transmission into art, since art appeals to human perception, which can be described with scientific theory. For Frank aesthetics is defined by the "cooperation between theory and experiment" (Piehler 2002: 239). Contrary to Helmar Frank he does not shy away from the idea of art, as it is voiced in his publication:

Today, aesthetics is offered new starting points; biological and technical aspects are added to its philosophical and historical aspects. For the first time the possibility of generally valid, verifiable statements about the phenomenon of art opens up. [...] The mathematical instrument of cybernetics is information theory. With it it has become possible for the first time to find a measure for that concept with the help of which a work of art can be recorded numerically: This term is information. (Frank 1984: 322)

Frank's theoretical approach to art strongly derives from cybernetics, and it operates with terms such as "structural data", "informational theory", and "redundancy". His artistic experiments at that time consisted of computer-generated images, which he named "Oszillogramme".

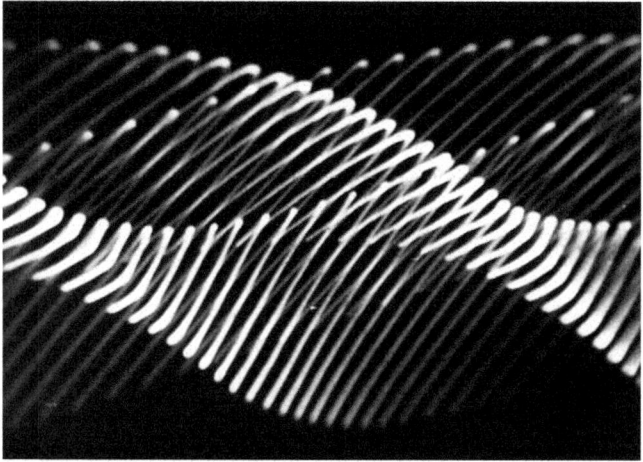

Fig. 3: H.W. Frank (1953): Oszillogramm

Frank's ideas and his images caused a wave of computer graphics, which had been produced by artists from about 1965 on, e.g. by the artists Frieder Nake and Georg Nees. The mathematician Nake, teaching at the Technical University Stuttgart (Technische Hochschule Stuttgart), developed a drawing software and a drawing machine "Graphomat Z64" which was connected to the institute's central computer. The "Graphomat" was operated with punch cards, and it could draw points and curves. Once again this artistic device was taken from a technological application: it had been designed for geodesy, meteorology and road construction (Herzogenrath/ Nierhoff-Wielk 2007: 236).

According to Frieder Nake, the production of a computer graphic turned out to be a highly complex procedure. A plotter read the perforated punch card and turned it into drawings, as Nake explains.

A brief press of the start button triggered the drawing process, which then proceeded automatically if no unforeseen disturbance occurred: exciting! What would the visual interpretation of the binary code of the pinhole strip produce and record as a line graphic? A date was written in September 1965. The world's third exhibition of computer art was being prepared. (Nake 2005: 47)

In his book on computer graphics, Nake makes a peculiar remark. In a footnote he comments upon a German television report, that a monkey was placed beside the Graphomat, somehow commenting on the artistic competence of artist and machine. Although this is a minor incidence, it speaks for the German attitude towards technological art as a whole, and, as has been mentioned, is still prevalent today (ibid.: 48).

Assessing the history of cybernetics and computer art, it has to be concluded that the US-American and German attitudes and practices highly differ. As has just been stated, the US-American experiments had been addressing social issues and met a welcoming attitude towards mass media and popular culture. Germany and the German art discourses kept some distance towards technolgoy, mass media and popular culture. This critical distance already existed towards the mass medium television and was then transferred to video art and other technical art forms (Hickethier 1994; Krewani 2001: 42-50). In a broader sense, Georg Bollenbeck notes the German bourgeoisie's critical distance from modernity (Bollenbeck 1994). This wider cultural context may account for the fact that computer graphics had not been given the space to develop, it was strictly restricted to Technical Universities.

The integration of digital art into the art system was brought about by the festival ars electronica since 1979 and the Zentrum für Kunst und Medien (ZKM) in Karlsruhe from 1989 on. Now the curating of computer art had found its place.

References

Ascott, Roy (2003): "Behaviourist Art and the Cybernetic Vision." Edward R. Shanken (ed.), Roy Ascott. Telematic Embrace. Visionary Theories of Art, Technology and Consciousness, Berkeley, Los Angeles: University of California Press, pp. 109–56.
Bense, Max (1956): Aesthetische Information. aesthetica II. Krefeld, Baden-Baden: Agis-Verlag.

Bense, Max (1998): "Einführung in die informationsästhetische Ästhetik." In: Max Bense (ed.) Ausgewählte Schriften: Bd. 3: Ästhetik und Texttheorie. Stuttgart: Agis-Verlag, pp. 251–417.

Bollenbeck, Georg (1994): Bildung und Kultur. Glanz und Elend eines deutschen Deutungsmusters. Frankfurt u. Leipzig.

Borck, Cornelius (2008): "Der Transhumanismus der Kontrollmaschine: Die Expo'67 als Vision einer kybernetischen Versöhnung von Mensch und Welt." In: Michael Hagner/Erich Hörl (eds.) Die Transformationen des Humanen. Beiträge zur Kulturgeschichte der Kybernetik. Frankfurt: Suhrkamp Verlag, pp. 125–62.

Cybernetic Serendipity. (https://monoskop.org/Cybernetic_Serendipity). Last Visit: Aug. 29, 2022.

Fernández, María (2008): "Gordon Pask: Cybernetic Polymath." In: Leonardo 41/2, pp. 163–168.

Franke, Herbert W. (1984): Computer Grafik. Galerie. Bilder nach Programm. Kunst im elektronischen Zeitalter. Köln: Du Mont Schauberg.

Hagner, Michael, Hörl, Erich (eds.) (2008): Die Transformation des Humanen. Beiträge zur Kulturgeschichte der Kybernetik. Frankfurt: Suhrkamp Verlag.

Hayles, Katherine N. (1999): How We Became Posthuman. Virtual Bodies in Cybernetics, Literature, and Informatics. Chicago, London: Univ. of Chicago Press.

Herzogenrath, Wulf, Nierhoff-Wielk, Barbara (eds.) (2007): Ex Machina—Frühe Computergrafik Bis 1979: Die Sammlungen Franke und weitere Stiftungen in der Kunsthalle Bremen; Herbert W. Franke Zum 80. Geburtstag; Kunsthalle Bremen 17. Juni Bis 26. August 2007 = Ex Machina—Early Computer Graphics up to 1979. With the help of H. W. Franke. München, Berlin: Deutscher Kunstverlag.

Hickethier, Knut (1994): "Das Fernsehspiel oder der Kunstanspruch der Erzählmaschine Fernsehen." In: Bernhard Zimmermann/Helmut Schanze (eds.), Geschichte des Fernsehens in der Bundesrepublik Deutschland, Bd.2. Das Fernsehen und die Künste. München: Wilhelm Fink Verlag, pp.303-348.

Hörl, Erich (2016): "Die Ökologisierung des Denkens." In: *ZfM Zeitschrift für Medienwissenschaft* 14/1, pp. 33–45.

Hörl, Erich, Hagner, Michael (2008): "Überlegungen zur kybernetischen Transformation des Humanen." In: Michael Hagner/Erich Hörl (eds.), Die Transformation des Humanen. Beiträge zur Kulturgeschichte der Kybernetik. Frankfurt: Suhrkamp Verlag, pp.7–37.

Hünnekens, Annette (1997): Der bewegte Betrachter: Theorien der interaktiven Medienkunst. Wienand Medien. Köln: Wienand.

Krewani, Angela (2001): Hybride Formen: New British Cinema—Television Drama—Hypermedia. Trier: Wissenschaftlicher Verlag Trier.

Krewani, Angela (2016): Medienkunst: Theorie—Praxis—Ästhetik. Trier: Wissenschaftlicher Verlag Trier.

McCray, W. Patrick (2022): "Art Out of Order: Jack Burnham, the 1970 Software Show, and the Aesthetics of Information Systems." In: Technology and Culture 63/3, pp. 689–717. https://doi.org/10.1353/tech.2022.0106.

McLuhan, Marshall (2003): Understanding Me: Lectures and Interviews. ed. with the help of Stephanie McLuhand/David Staines, Toronto, Ont. McClelland.

Mersch, Dieter (2019): "Kreativität und Künstliche Intelligenz. Einige Bemerkungen zu einer Kritik algorithmischer Rationalität." In: ZfM Zeitschrift für Medienwissenschaft 11/2, pp. 65–74. https://doi.org/10.25969/MEDIAREP/12634.

Müller, Albert (2008): "Zur Geschichte der Kybernetik. Ein Zwischenstand." In: Österreichische Zeitschrift für Geisteswissenschaften 19/4, pp. 6–27.

Nake, Frieder (2005): "Und wann endlich 'Kunst'—oder doch lieber nicht?" In: Claus Pias, ed. Zukünfte des Computers, 47–66. Berlin: diaphanes, pp. 47-66.

Pias, Claus (2008): "'Hollerith 'gefiederter' Kristalle'. Kunst, Wissenschaft und Computer in Zeiten der Kybernetik." In: Michael Hagner/Erich Hörl (eds.), Die Transformation des Humanen. Beiträge zur Kulturgeschichte der Kybernetik. Frankfurt: Suhrkamp Verlag, pp.72–106.

Pickering, Andrew (2002): "Cybernetics and the Mangle: Ashby, Beer and Pask." In: Social Studies of Science 32/3, pp. 413–37.

Piehler, Heike (2002): Die Anfänge der Computerkunst. Frankfurt/Main: dot-Verl. Dr. Dotzler Medien-Institut. Zugl. Kiel, Univ., Diss., 2000.

Scorzin, Pamela (2021): "Kann KI Kunst sein? AI ART: Neue Positionen, technisierte Ästhetiken von Mensch und Maschine. In: Kunstforum International 278/4, p 48.

Shamberg, Michael (1971): Guerilla Television. New York, Chicago: Holt, Rinehart and Winston.

Shanken, Edward (2001): "From Cybernetics to Telematics: The Art, Pedagogy, And Theory Of Roy Ascott". In: Edward A. Shanken, ed. Telematic Embrace: Visionary Theories of Art, Technology and Consciousness by Roy Ascott. University of California Press. pp.ii-x.

Simondon, Gilbert (1980) [1958]: On the Mode of Existence of Technological Objects. Ontario: University of Western Ontario. Preface by John Hart.

Turner, Fred (2008): From Counterculture to Cyberculture: Stewart Brand, the Whole Earth Network, and the Rise of Digital Utopianism. Paperback ed. Chicago, Ill. Univ. of Chicago Pr.

Youngblood, Gene (1970): Expanded Cinema. New York: Dutton.

A Slightly Off Performance
Some Observations on Algorithmic Translation as/in Artistic Practice

Anna Luhn

Abstract

This article deals with questions of utilisation and implementation of algorithmic translation techniques within contemporary artistic practice. Loosely departing from two particular artworks, Baden Pailthorpe's Lingua Franca *and Julia Nakotte's* #file.read()*, I aim at an understanding of the role translation technology might or might not play within the realm of contemporary textual/digital arts, as well as getting a grasp on how artworks incorporating machine translation (MT) technology might inform current re-conceptualisations of (literary) translation. Contextualising contemporary artistic practice with the historical foundations and early reception of MT as well as with recent developments of large language models, I hope to contribute to a first speculative general framing of the utilisation of machine translation techniques within artistic practice.*

Keywords

Machine Translation, Language Art, Digital Art, Avant-garde Poetics, ChatGPT, Originality, Algorithmic Creation, Artistic Genre, Translation, Baden Pailthorpe, Julia Nakotte, Warren Weaver

The following thoughts circle around the utilisation and implementation of algorithmic translation[1] techniques within contemporary artistic practice, or, if you wish, around current translation techniques within the context of algorithmic art

---

1 If not otherwise stated, I refer here to *interlingual* translation, i.e., the translation of a word, a phrase, or a text from one linguistic entity, qualified as 'source language', into another linguistic entity, defined as 'target language'. Research for this article was funded by the Deutsche Forschungsgemeinschaft (DFG, German Research Foundation) under Germany's Excellence Strategy in the context of the Cluster of Excellence Temporal Communities: Doing Literature in a Global Perspective – EXC 2020 – Project ID 390608380.

practice. Loosely departing from two particular artworks, these reflections are to be understood as a first attempt at developing a more general understanding of the role translation technology might or might not play in the (textual, literary, digital) arts and what (textual, literary, digital) artworks using this technology bring to current re-conceptualisations of translation. By tracing a loose arc from current artistic practice to the historical foundations and reception of machine translation (MT) to recent algo-linguistic developments, I hope to contribute to a broader contextualisation of their relation, to shed light on some of its forms and thus to give the utilisation of MT within artistic practice a first speculative framing.

Let me start with a short description of two more or less recent artworks that exploit, or include, algorithmic translation in their creation in comparable ways—even if the status and role allocated to the technology may differ significantly in the respective works. *Lingua Franca*, an artwork by media artist Baden Pailthorpe originating from 2011, gravitates around a technologically effectuated 'translation loop' of George Orwell's 1949 dystopian classic *Nineteen Eighty-Four*. Pailthorpe uses the algorithmic translator *Google translate* to convert the novel successively into all 58 languages provided by the online translation service at the time of the artwork's creation, before letting the algorithms translate the translated text back into English. A general audience could learn of the newly created "experimental literary work" brought to life by this "extended process of linguistic remixing",[2] as the documenting peritext on the artists' website framed the work, via Pailthorpe's Twitter account @EightyFourDoors, where snippets of it were posted from November 18th, 2011 to January 23rd, 2012. Giving a good impression of the textual sound of the work, the first four posts read: "April that recognized three times", "The application of the colour of a great seems to be against.", "Paper dust by the wind a little amount of damage, the women vortex street the sun is shining the sky blue," "it's difficult to paint with all things in any way."[3] The complete text of this 'new', algorithmically produced version (which could as well be called a translation, or a parody or a pastiche) of the novel *Nineteen Eighty-Four* was then turned into a hardcover publication titled *Eighty-four Doors*, as such being materialised as a book in its own right with a proper ISBN.

#file.read() is a 2021 artwork by Julia Nakotte that consists of three algorithmically generated poems à five stanzas, initially published in the fourth issue of the German journal *Kurze*. In the publication, Nakotte provides the fully executable computer script alongside the poems, *face à face*. To arrive at the three poems,

---

2   https://www.badenpailthorpe.com/#/lingua-franca/

3   See https://twitter.com/eightyfourdoors/status/148280331437477889?s=21&t=Xbw w3EZ6k3dqE7l9soH4lA; https://twitter.com/eightyfourdoors/status/14828362098 8157952?s=21&t=Xbww3EZ6k3dqE7l9soH4lA; https://twitter.com/eightyfourdoors/status/148285592352997376?s=21&t=Xbww3EZ6k3dqE7l9soH4lA; https://twitter.com/eightyfourdoors/status/148285721315246080?s=21&t=Xbww3EZ6k3dqE7l9so H4lA (all posted on November 18, 2011).

"Sinn", "auf," and "Freunde", the artist wrote a short program that was run once to generate the three texts. According to the script, for each of the poems, Nakotte's program chose randomly, five times, several words out of a German word corpus comprising the entire third issue of *Kurze*. The program then ran the generated verses through an algorithmic translation into Japanese, into English, and then back into German again. The results, in this case the generated poem "Sinn" (Engl. *sense*, also: *meaning*), would read like this:

Ich bin schon voll
er
    Kein Staubwedel
Ich habe den Zähler hier gelassen
Wenn es Spaß gemacht hat, war ich es nicht
Ich bin im Garten nebenan[4]
              (Nakotte 2021:33)

Both Pailthorpe and Nakotte are utilising algorithmic translation technology in their work in a similar way, in that they employ it as a form of looping technique, starting with linguistic material in a particular language and coming back to that same language after several translational detours via other languages (two in the case of Nakotte, 58 in the case of Pailthorpe). Both works could therefore be said to perform, using the term of Roman Jakobson's seminal distinction between the three elemental forms of translation, several *interlingual translations* as well as a (final) *intralingual translation*.[5] They nevertheless mark, I would argue, two poles within the spectrum of possible ways to implement algorithmic translation within artistic practice, a point to which I will return later.

Early Machine Translation and Artistic Indifference

The use of algorithmic translation techniques within textual or other artistic practices has not been of particularly great interest so far within the context of the quickly growing scholarly occupation with digital artistic practice, spanning its research on "writing in programmable and networked media" (Cayley 2018: 148)

---

4   ("I am already full / he [/] No feather duster / I left the counter here / If it was fun, it was not me / I am in the garden next-door").

5   In his influential essay "Linguistic Aspects on Translation", Jakobson distinguishes between three types of translation: interlingual translation (or: "translation proper") is performed between two distinct languages, interlingual translation (or: "rewording") reformulates a text within the realm of one sole language, intersemiotic translation (or: "transmutation") interprets verbal signs by means of non-verbal signs (e.g.: text to film), cf. Jakobson 1959: 233.

from the tracing of its roots and predecessors in mid-century algorithmic art or pre-digital avant-garde practices at the beginning of the 20th century to its contemporary integration of so-called 'artificial intelligence' (or, broadly put, machine learning) and its critical engagement with it. The most prominently discussed examples of textual technology as/in artistic practice are undoubtedly not linked to algorithmic translation but to 'free' algorithmic generative text production.[6] The relative lack of interest is remarkable insofar as the relation between MT and contemporary text-based/literary digital art is closer than one might initially assume. On the one hand, historically: within the development of algorithmic technology, MT has always been the most 'avant-garde' of computational practice. At the beginning of the 1960s, talking about algorithmic translation techniques was quasi-tantamount to discussing the changes of "language in the technical age," as the title of German Journal *Sprache im technischen Zeitalter*, founded by literary critic Walter Höllerer, stated boldly. In its first issue in 1961, the first ever article of *Sprache im technischen Zeitalter* was accordingly devoted to a discussion of recent developments in MT by the Austrian computer pioneer Heinz Zemanek, evaluating "the possibilities and limits of automatic language translation" (Zemanek 1961: 3)[7] based on the latest research available to him. If it seemed imperative to talk about the conditions and the "necessary draw on and resistance of language in a century influenced by technology,"(Höllerer 1961: 1) i.e., a century facing computerisation and utopias and fears of the human-like machine alike; if it was deemed more than an urgent undertaking to talk about the modifications that human language underwent from the mid-century onwards and the heavy changes implied in its utilisation and its theorisation—and that decidedly included the use of poetic language as well—, the first and most important field to look at was the development of machine translation. Christine Mitchell (2018) sums it up well: "it's significant that MT is often held up—despite its consistently capricious yield—as the most basic example of Artificial Intelligence; their conceptions and fortunes are linked."[8]

---

6   Rita Raley is one of the few scholars that have taken a closer look to multiple forms of algorithmic translation within artistic contexts, discussing in detail various examples of media art deploying MT technology, including the above-mentioned Pailthorpe work, cf. Raley 2016.

7   The above given quote formed the title of Zemanek's essay: "Möglichkeiten und Grenzen der automatischen Sprachübersetzung", published in *Sprache im technischen Zeitalter* 1 (1961). Hannes Bajohr discusses Zemaneks contribution to the first issue of *Sprache im technischen Zeitalter* within the Walter Höllerer lecture 2022, held at Technische Universität Berlin on December 9, 2022 (Bajohr 2022).

8   The special issue "Translation-Machination" of the online journal *Amodern*, edited by Rita Raley and Christine Mitchell, provides an impressive compilation of relevant voices and perspectives on the topic and has been an invaluable source for the above reflections.

What, then, are the theoretical foundations of modern "computer translation," as Warren Weaver dubbed the not-yet developed technology in his groundlaying memorandum of machine translation development? In 1949, Weaver prepared a short manuscript for the Rockefeller Foundation entitled *Translation*, which outlined the basic idea of a computer-based translation process. Weaver's ideas were based on the principles of cryptography developed during World War II.[9] In twelve typewritten pages, he explored the potentials and difficulties of a future "computer translation" based on the heuristic assumption that a language to translate from (generally referred to as 'source language' within the context of translation studies) could be understood as *encryption* that simply needed to be decoded. The paper laid the foundation for the triumph of algorithmic translation. Initially resisted by Norbert Wiener, to whom Weaver submitted his early sketches in an exchange of letters, the ideas of computer-aided machine translation soon fell on fertile ground. As early as the 1950s, its development was massively promoted in various state-funded research projects fuelled by the military and industrial sectors. First development stages aimed at the creation and perfection of a rule-based machine translation (RBMT): These systems, developed by computer specialists with the help of linguists, initially translated word by word with the aid of codified dictionaries; grammatical rule systems, which, for example, regulated the position or repositioning of certain word groups in the translation output, were soon added. As early as 1955, the Massachusetts Institute of Technology published an anthology with fourteen practical essays on the state of the art of algorithmic translation under the title *Machine Translation of Languages*, edited by William N. Locke of MIT and A. Donald Booth of the Birkbeck College Computation Laboratory in London, with a foreword by Weaver himself that bore the meaningful title *The New Tower*.

Already in his 1949 memorandum, Weaver had used a modified 'Tower of Babel' metaphor, by which he had imagined different languages as a collection of large, inhabited, but closed towers built over a common foundation:

When they [the individuals living in the towers] try to communicate with one another they shout back and forth, each from his own closed tower. It is difficult to make the sound penetrate even the nearest towers, and communication proceeds very poorly indeed. But when an individual goes down his tower, he finds himself in a great open basement, common to all the towers. Here he establishes easy and useful communication with the persons who have also descended from their towers. (Weaver 1949: 11)

Starting from the speculation of an underlying structure common to all human languages, reminiscent of Chomsky's theorems of generative transformation

---

9   For a detailed "archeology" of machine translation and its roots in cryptographic techniques, cf. DuPoint 2018.

grammar (which indeed were soon to become one of the most important pillars of computational linguistics), Weaver in *Translation* even spoke of a "real but yet undiscovered universal language" as the "common base of human communication." (Weaver 1949: 11)

As those grounding metaphors and images show all too blatantly, the basic linguistic assumption underlying the first steps in the development of machine translation was the old dualism between form and gist/content, presenting itself in new information-theoretical ways. "In its broadest sense the subject of this volume of essays can be described as the completely automatic substitution of a different language for the language of a given text, the ideas being kept unchanged," as Boothe and Locke (1955: 1) formulated it in their *Machine Translation of Languages*. In line with Weaver's cryptographic point of departure, computational linguistic research was, from the start, dominated by the notion of language systems as code systems that, in the ideal of machine translation, could (or should be able to) be mapped perfectly and ultimately onto each other. The conception embedded in this idea of a linguistically and textually expressible 'sense', transportable across language systems without damage or loss via algorithmic translation technology, is that of *translation-as-vehicle*. 'Translation' understood in this way describes a medium by which content can circulate on a global scale within specific distribution pathways and independently of the linguistic system in which it was originally composed. From such a conception follows the ideal state of a translated text, where—content-wise—the intended ending point of a translation procedure could be completely synonymous with its starting point, a circular pattern in which original and translation would ultimately become indistinguishable with regard to the assumed intrinsic 'meaning'.[10]

Concerning the early computer linguists' predictions on the future use and applicability of mechanical translation in the field of *artistic*, i.e., literary or poetic practice, Weaver had been more than sceptical in his initial memorandum. But, opposed to his verdict that mechanical translation would never be able to achieve "elegance and style," (Weaver 1949: 7) Booth and Locke were, already in their introduction to the 1955 essay collection, quite optimistic about the creation of a "machine with a sufficiently extensive storage organ [that] would be able to

---

10   In this context, then prominent considerations about a machine interlanguage (also: 'pivot language' or 'machinese'), an artificial language that was meant to be interposed in the translation process between two languages in order to replace bilingual machine translation systems by a universally applicable system, seem to be a logical consequence of the ideal of maximum codifiability of language. Statistical machine translation technology (SMT), which was first used by IBM in the 1980s and successively replaced RBMT, still uses this method today. For a rough historical overview of the developmental steps within the MT field from rule-based to statistical to neural machine translation, see, for example, Kenny 2018.

construct rhymes and rhythms and to relate these to the ideas contained in the original text, provided only that the necessary additional cues to sound, syllable structures, and stress were provided in the memory with suitable routines for processing them."(Locke/Booth 1955: 14) On the other side of the North Pole, Soviet linguists Isaac Revzin and Viktor Rosenzweig explicitly addressed the prospect of including literary translation in the portfolio of future algorithmic translation technology, bringing into play in this context a possible mediation via 'interlanguage' even for non-mechanical human translation practice. (Revzin/Rosenzweig 1964)

Confronted with the new player in the field of textual and translational creation, critical reactions that arose out of the literary and intellectual-academic sphere predominantly pointed to the field's grounding equation of language and code. The theoretical assumption of an existing or potentially achievable 'semantic synonymity' between languages—be it implicitly or explicitly formulated within MT's theoretical foundations—formed the main point of concern for a number of scholars and intellectuals following the first steps, successes and defeats of MT in the 1960s and 70s.[11] Emergent in a decidedly political era, their criticism was unsurprisingly profoundly rooted in primarily leftist political argumentation. The fear of a world where linguistic structures and properties of languages would be made fitting to the requirements of an economically driven machine logic of language, where languages would be made literally *exchangeable*, was synonymous with the fear of a world where such forms of language technology would not only lead to an impoverishment of language in general but to its commodification: a commodified language for a commodified people.

In this regard, the development of machine translation was met by the proponents of avant-garde poetics as well as avant-garde theorists with remarkably less enthusiasm than other texto-lingual possibilities that were opened up by the fast progress within computer development. Theo Lutz's famous stochastic texts based on a corpus of Kafka's novels, Oulipo's interest in algorithmic text generation and Max Bense's *Informationsästhetik* (German for: Aesthetics of Information) are but three examples of a widespread hope for an all-new post-war aesthetics in avant-garde philosophy and literary theory of the time and the heavy influence of information theory on the humanities (cf. Cramer 2011: 185ff.)[12] But, other than the newly discovered possibility of generating poetic textuality out of the machine's heart and (at least almost) without human intervention, the arrival of algorithmic *translation* did not spark particular inspiration among poets. Avant-garde transla-

---

11   For selected intellectual perspectives on translation and machination within the late 1960s, cf. Luhn 2022: 32ff.
12   Obviously, those early experiments and approaches were also subject to scepticism, critique and objections: All gloom, Paul Celan diagnoses the arrival of "cybernetic poetry" as the end of all poetic conversation as early as 1960 (cf. Gellhaus 1997: 399).

tional experimentation was done elsewhere, often in implicit or explicit rejection of the new technology's linguistic-machinist basis (cf. Luhn 2022: ch. 1, 2).

In an attempt to explain this lack of artistic interest in the then-new technology, one might be tempted to conclude that, historically, MT was simply not developed enough in the 1960s and 70s to facilitate artistic experimentation or avant-garde exploration in a profound way. And maybe the same could even be claimed, less boldly though, for our current time. But this explanation does not stand on solid ground, for the similarity, at least of the textual results of some experimental/activist translational practice and mechanical translation procedures, has long been noted (cf. Mitchell 2010: 25). Moreover, one could convincingly argue that an emerging technology's lack of maturity has never really been an issue for whichever artistic experimentation or movement adopting it. If the topic or question of translation technology has always been quite a bit off regarding, on the one hand, artistic integration and, on the other hand, the discussion of algorithmic technology within the context of artistic practice, the reason may very well not be found in the specifics of translation *technology* but in the particular and problematic status of literary translation *as artistic text practice* as such. All through history, poetic translation has been qualified by the vast majority as a purely derivative act. Its status as an original art has been contested or denied, or, in all honesty, it was never really on the table, even before putting a machine in the loop. That is: poetic translation is and has been seen generally by the majority of scholars and 'laymen' alike (though not by professional literary translators) first and foremost as a secondary practice by which an original work (its 'content', its 'gist') in a certain language is transferred into another linguistic system by making sure to keep the specific style or tone intact as much as possible. Literary translation is then understood as a facilitator of *transmission*—an understanding that, in the 1960s discussions, even drew theoretical inspiration from machine translation's intellectual surroundings, from communication or information theory.[13] It may or may not be a coincidence, then, that the first genuinely influential attempts to question the hierarchy between 'original' poetic texts and their translations, or at least the elevation of poetic translation to an equivalent status as poetic creation, to an art in its own right, fall within the time of the first popularisation of mechanical translation. Suddenly, the foundations and framing of the ancient cultural technique seem at stake or at least negotiable; and so they are negotiated, for example within the Brazilian avant-garde group *Noigandres*, or within other contexts of often avantgarde-related experimentative translation practice and theory in the 1960s.[14]

---

13 In the 1960s, a number of influential scholars occupied with the topic of literary translation refer in their research directly to concepts of communication theory, among them Eugene Nida and Jiří Levý.
14 For a 'cannibalogical' conception of literary translation as a resistant practice in the context of the Brazilian *Noigandres*, see, for example, Strasser 2020.

In the course of the institutionalisation of 'Translation Studies' in the 1970s and the establishment of critical translation theory, questions of hierarchisation and definition were heavily discussed, within the context of feminist and postcolonial theory strands from the 1980s on (cf. Chamberlain 1988). If those pushes led to a more nuanced evaluation of the procedures and practices of the different forms and types of translation within the specialists' field, the perception of the general public, I would argue, has not changed much until recently. Mainly, translation, may it or may it not be in artistic contexts, is seen in connection to a regime of functionality: literary translation as an instrument, a practice, a medium for providing and guaranteeing the circulation of textual artworks in other linguistic contexts than that of their origins. Machine translation does not *produce* this conception—even if the pseudo-cryptographic rooting and the computational linguistic understanding of language as a zero-sum game of equivalence indeed solidify such a perspective on literary translational practice. However, the technology of machine translation *does* put a bright spotlight on the ever-liminal position, the ever-precarious status of poetic translation as a cultural practice that tends to be made or even to make itself invisible (Venuti 1995/2008). If a 2015 New York Times article about the latest developments in algorithmic translation could have the headline "Is translation an art or a math problem?" (Lewis-Kraus 2015), most definitely no scholar in or outside the literary field, no critic, no random person would ever put forward an equivalent question with regard to a textual practice such as poetry or novel writing—at least that was true for the now-ending era preceding the (media) triumph of large language models (LLM) in the context of 'imaginative' text generation.

Artificial text creation and questions of originality

In light of various major LLM releases in the early 2020s, one could observe certain hopes, fears and lines of argumentation from the last third of the 20th century recur in regard to the two areas of algorithmic textuality described above, that is, algorithmic translation technology and 'free' generative text production. At the end of November 2022, the US-American company OpenAI released their newest large language model based on neural language processing (NLP): ChatGPT, the acronym GPT standing for *Generative Pre-trained Transformer*. The chatbot, equipped with 'artificial intelligence', could interact with users and generate texts to conform to their demands. Before Christmas, countless articles, analyses, think pieces and critical essays had flooded the international press not only in technology sections but also in every possibly related newspaper section, be it Politics, feuilleton, or Society. Using an improved version of the language model GPT-3, which had already sparked notable but significantly less public attention upon its release in 2020, the prototype ChatGPT created immense hype within a very short time, with millions of users trying it out and generating tons of gratis testing data for the providing company. The awe and astonishment verbalised in almost all journalistic branches was accompanied by lead articles that expressed strong unease at the perfection with which ChatGPT could simulate coherent text production without any content- or style-related limitations. At the core of its critical journalistic assessment lay basically only one paraphrasable question: 'Will ChatGPT be the AI that changes everything?'[15]

The sinister undertones of its media coverage are but one sign of the latest LLMs' considerable potential for shaking up not only educational environments, marketing branches or the scientific publishing field; because ChatGPT will, if asked to do so, not only produce astonishingly coherent-sounding seminar papers, encyclopaedia entries or advertisement blurbs. The spectrum also includes fully executable computer code, correctly rhymed and metrically trimmed sonnets and fictional text adventures. ChatGPT can tell stories and write poetry or (to summarize the complex technology in a very superficial fashion) it could be described as being able to *simulate* fictional narrating and poeticising on the grounds of statistics and massive data sets combined with the technological ability to memorise and 'learn' from previous decisions. The floor is open to paranoid or—depending on the standpoint—jubilatory anticipation. Is the so-called 'AI' or, more precisely, are deep-learning large language models preparing for a leap into the artistic sphere and will human-made poetic textuality, in the very near future, stand in competition with 'artificial literature' that rivals us in our originality?[16]

---

15   A few out of numerous examples from German and English language newspapers from 2022: *New York Times* discusses the topic under the headline " The New Chatbots Could Change the World. Can You Trust Them?", German newspaper *tageszeitung* asks: "Artificial Intelligence via ChatGPT: Everything changed?" *Der Spiegel* diagnoses that "ChatGPT marks the end of irrelevant artificial intelligence." *The Guardian* titles: " What is AI chatbot phenomenon ChatGPT and could it replace humans?" (https://www.nytimes.com/2022/12/10/technology/ai-chat-bot-chatgpt.html; https://taz.de/Kuenstliche-Intelligenz-via-ChatGpT/!5903102/"; https://www.spiegel.de/netzwelt/web/chatgpt-markiert-das-ende-der-irrelevanten-kuenstlichen-intelligenz-kolumne-a-b2afeb69-083d-4e69-8920-da5cad549d5f; https://www.theguardian.com/technology/2022/dec/05/what-is-ai-chatbot-phenomenon-chatgpt-and-could-it-replace-humans).

16   As for the literary sector, writers have been quick to include the technology within their artistic practice, to tackle it by responding to it, integrating it, or bending it, producing co-authored publications. See, for example, the following publications of NLP-including literary works by K Allado-MacDowell, *Pharmako-AI* and *Amor Cringe*; Mattis Kuhn, *Selbstgespräche mit einer KI* (2021), and David Jhave Johnston, *ReRites* (2019), consisting of human as well as on-human writing—besides a more conventional application of the technology I am not excluding in this paper, that is, its exploitation in the lines of 'letting the AI do the artistic/creative work for me' or 'making writing (genre) fiction easier with the help of AI'. The web is booming with 'how to'-manuals. See for example these instructions to get ChatGPT to write poems

While undoubtedly having been openly accessible for non-specialist users for much longer than generative language models like GPT, deep learning machine translation has not been able to create an even comparable media storm in recent history.[17] Neither has it, apart, maybe, from some experts' conversations within professional circles, been seen to produce similar dooming cries of warning about the end of the *raison d'être* of human creativity or originality. That is not to say that there have not been critical voices regarding the political implications and economic conditions underlying its ubiquity, as well as discussions about its limits of applicability, general quality issues, environmental concerns and ethical problems: be it in light of its roots in wartime cryptography and its development within cold war objectives (Slater 2018) or be it with a critical linguistic perspective on biased output and the 'leveling' of languages in the wake of its more and more extensive use in a growing number of fields (Raley 2003; Apter 2006; Gramling 2016; Bender 2021).[18]

If deep learning MT nevertheless 'fails' to create comparable panic over the impending end of originality as humanity's 'unique selling point' due to the abilities of the text-providing GPT-'family' or—in the realm of fine art—neural networks-based programs like DALL-E or Stable Diffusion[19], the reason may be connected to a difference in its primary goals and historical setting. Though undoubtedly a cold war brainchild, MT's first conceptual stages by Weaver were laid out with a particular *ethos* in mind: the (admittedly economically motivated) wish to establish communication without (language) borders, to minimise the effort of reproducing textual entities (scientific papers, contracts, manuals, etc.)

---

in a certain style, even including specific demands regarding meter and rhyme (https://medium.com/@Pawel.Sierszen/structuring-creativity-poetry-generation-with-chatgpt-e7ffb4568196). Subscription services promise to their users the ability to "painlessly construct unique stories, thrilling tales, seductive romances" with the help of their generative language technology (https://novelai.net/). For a critical reportage on the mounting number of mostly genre writers including generative text technology in their writing, see Dzieza 2022.

17 The very first version of Google translate went online in 2006, the much-praised deepL Translator was released in 2017.

18 Nuanced research is pursued steadily in the context of Translation Studies, where CAT (computer-aided translation) figures as a long-standing topic and field of interest. The sector of literary or poetic translation has been thought, until now, quite immune to the recent growing discourse on algorithmic machine translation, or at least confident to stand up to it: besides the fact that translation of poetic genres, routed in a complex entanglement of cultural, literary and aesthetic knowledge as well as familiarity with the respective authors, seems conceptually inherently unfitting to automated, consciousness-less translation processes, results have not been very satisfactory until now, cf. for a recent overview on the topic Brodersen 2022.

19 Note of the editors: cf. the article of Marco Donnarumma in this issue of the journal.

within different linguistic systems and to facilitate global understanding. In comparison, ChatGPT's scope and its ability to provide quasi-perfect *simulations* of coherent and genre-proof text production in any given field and context seems an offence to the status of human brain-work by its sheer conceptual set-up: because the *only* goal one can imagine for such a capability is the ultimate replacement of the human writer, scholar or texter by a "nonhuman, limitless linguistic generativity to come." (Slater 2018: unpaginated)

As this *effect* might just as well come true for translation technology based on artificial neural networks (ANN), unquestionably improving at an enormous speed, it is not comparably valid for the 'ideological' grounding of the technology itself. But an even stronger factor for MT's 'failure' to threaten originality as a last human resort is, I would argue, precisely rooted in the problematic status of literary translation as such within the conceptual realm of artistically framed, that is, original or creative, textual production, as stated above. As an effect of its liminality, while text creation via generative language models is discussed within the *cadre* of originality and creativity, the results of translation technology simply are not: they are inextricably bound to the framework of functionality, seen through the lens of 'accuracy', whether it be claimed that this accuracy can only be achieved by impoverishing languages through a one-to-one equivalence principle, forming a global "glossodiverse monolingualism" (Gramling 2016: 38) in the long run, or be it in the sense that translation technology is simply not (yet) capable (enough) of producing translations as 'good' as those produced by human translators.

Translation as a genre shifter and a shifting genre

What does, then, to come back to my two initial examples, the constantly contested status of translation as an artistic practice, the precarious position of 'translating' as an original art, mean in regard to the implementation of MT techniques *as/in* contemporary artistic practices? Firstly, MT in artistic contexts brings forward, or 'induces', a shift of genre, a fact that differentiates this particular type of implementation of computational technology from the application of other algorithmic procedures incorporated into artistic creation. Whereas, in the framework of the arts, algorithmic generative writing is generally introduced or included to produce *writing*, framed as (algorithmic) language art, poetry, or fiction, and algorithmically managed image production is typically executed to create *images*, framed as (algorithmic) art, one could hardly state the same as confidently for algorithmic translation procedures performed in the context of (as such verbalised) artistic practices, resulting in a specific artwork. More concretely: For the two works mentioned above by Pailthorpe and Nakotte, it seems strangely off to claim that they integrate algorithmic translation in their artistic practice to produce a *'translation'*. Both Pailthorpe and Nakotte handle and produce something they identify with the genre of poetic text production—poetry in the case of Nakotte, "literary work[s]" in the case of Pailthorpe. Nevertheless, what is traditionally termed 'literary translation' (a recreation of a foreign language text in another language that is as 'truthful' as possible for the sake of its dissemination) reflects neither the essence nor the goal of their works. This conceptual shift is already hinted at by the circumstance that their respective artistic creations begin and end with poetic material written in the same language. Machine translation processes seem to function here more as a way of installing a *detour*, an alienation process from the initial textual material, separated firstly from the consciousness of the artists and secondly from *any* human consciousness.

The very cursory description of the two artworks provided at the beginning of this article should suffice to grasp how Pailthorpe's and Nakotte's approach to MT, as well as the nature and set-up of *Lingua Franca* and *#file.read()*, differ nevertheless significantly from each other. Very heuristically, one could take the individual artworks as paradigmatic examples for two 'types' of MT-utilising media art resulting in digital literary text-work. The first type could be described as diving critically into the recent algo-technological developments via their practice, the second type as integrating them neatly into a digital artistic score without further (at least visible) critical assessment of the technology used. Belonging to the first type, Pailthorpe's *Lingua Franca* appears as a pertinent artwork of a generation of media artists, who are in Rita Raley's words "exploring the aesthetic and sociopolitical dimensions of machine and automatic translation practices, artists presenting us with self-reflexive representations and enactments of translational procedures," offering "models of critical engagement with the new linguistic doxa." (Raley 2016: 126, 134) In the artist's accompanying statement, *Lingua Franca*'s critical engagement with the ubiquitous presence of linguistic algorithms in the digitised age is made explicit. In the peritext to his artwork, Pailthorpe states that "in the age of software, code is the contemporary lingua franca" and that, at each of the stages of the algorithmic translation process, "the 'voices' of Google's algorithms become more and more present in the translations. Words are omitted, the syntax is rearranged, and new words are added. Indeed, a machinic sub-language rapidly emerges, emancipated from the confines of its interface."

But even without providing a contextualising commentary, the artist's critical engagement could be guessed from the combination of the artistic proceedings and the literary work Pailthorpe chose to put through the process. If it seems very unlikely, anyhow, that George Orwell's *Nineteen Eighty-Four* could have been a random pick, Pailthorpe's related notes confirm the critical implication of this choice, referring to the "political power of language"[20] as an already core topic of Orwell's dystopian world classic. In this context, it is decisive that Pailthorpe's work is putting a spotlight on the deficiency of 2012 language technology, which fails to adequately grapple with the delicate fabric of linguistically shaped semantic

---

20 All quotes from https://www.badenpailthorpe.com/#/lingua-franca/.

textures, though accidentally producing moments of unexpected poeticity: The short summary on the @EightyFourDoors Twitter account comments on this failure by framing the artwork that results from the artistic-algorithmic procedures as "Linguistic remix. Shit translation. Beautiful errors."[21] And it is all the more remarkable in this regard that, by evaluating the newly created "experimental literary work" in terms of translational accuracy, Pailthorpe is referencing the historically powerful mainstream narrative of translation as a linguistic transposal of a given 'original' that should be as smooth as possible. In doing so, he lets his *Lingua Franca* remain within the traditional frame of translational concepts, following the often implicit doxa that a good translation, in comparison to a "shitty" one, is one that would not make (even "beautiful") mistakes.

In stark contrast to *Lingua Franca*'s evident grounding in an artistic-critical engagement with the sociopolitical implications of an algorithmically shaped linguistic globality, Nakotte's *#file.read()*—a 'multiple' algorithmic artwork that combines code writing with algorithmic text generation and the use of algorithmic translation—does not exhibit a particular interest in the critique of machine translation techniques, if any at all. If the utilisation and nature of algorithmic translation technology have been an issue of concern within the artwork's fundamentals or Nakotte's artistic process, this reflection does not show in the final poetic publication. 'Translation' is not, as is the case with Pailthorpe, the *topic* of Nakotte's work; in a very unsophisticated way, one could describe it as a mere *technique* that she uses in order to get to her envisioned result: three automatically generated poems. The integration of MT, then, is apparent only through the published code, leaving the reader of the provided script in the dark regarding Nakotte's motivation to let the program execute the three translational steps (Ger -> En -> Ja -> Ger) in the process of generating the poetic output. As a result, the algorithmic translation procedures of *#file.read()* can be perceived solely in the framework of idiosyncratic, if not arbitrary artistic choice. Do the chosen languages have a point of reference in the initial word corpus? Could the artist have chosen more (or fewer) translational steps? Is it crucial that the translation was executed after the random choosing of the words or would it also have been possible to 'triple-translate' the whole corpus before algorithmically collecting the 15 stanzas? No answers are provided or deducible from the final result; the artist's choice to integrate algorithmic translation in the process of her digital art creation remains completely enigmatic.

What follows from this is a remarkable shift in the conceptual framing of 'translation' as a cultural practice as such: Whereas Pailthorpe remains, with his take on and application of algorithmic translation, within the limits of a mainstream conceptualisation of translation, within which he *must* stay in order to be able to make a valuable critique through his artistic work, Nakotte's approach

---

21   Cf. https://twitter.com/eightyfourdoors.

could be described as a deliberate ignorance of the technology's functional *cadre:* in a certain sense (mis-)using the technology, her artistic codework strips the functionality of the culturally handed-down and in this case algorithmically executed technique traditionally called 'translation'. What is left, then, is an executed performance of transforming linguistic entities belonging to a particular language system into other linguistic entities belonging to another language system and doing that by certain rules (semantically grounded in human practice, statistically bound in algorithmic procedures). By using algorithmic translation in such a hermetic way, refusing a hermeneutical as well as a critical resolution, *#file.read()* leaves the framework of reference traditionally linked to the concept of translation behind, whereas it is necessarily maintained in Pailthorpe's critical assessment of the new globalised language regime brought forward by algorithmic power. Nakotte's 'senseless' appropriative digestion of algorithmic translation technology leaves us with a non-rationalisable artistic practice in its own right, with no accessible entry point for its judgment via categories such as 'sufficiency' or 'accuracy'.

Holding Nakotte's and Pailthorpe's artistic employment of algorithmic translation technology against each other, both types of artworks can provide, in a very different way, an inherently critical perspective on the premises and promises of algorithmic translation and, put more broadly, of techno-linguistic conditionality: Pailthorpe by making it the topical and discursive core of his work, Nakotte by creolising it. Operating on yet another level, the two types of artistic engagement have in common that their proceedings make the practice of (literary) translation visible *as such*, be it via peritext or open codework. In doing so, both works hollow out the still (despite all criticism against it) dominant paradigm and dogma of its invisibility, the phantasma of its undisruptive functioning, its 'immateriality'. Even if, at first sight, it seems at odds with the *machine* in automated translation processes, it is precisely in working with algorithmic translation technology that *Lingua Franca* and *#file.read()* stage poetic translation as a decidedly original, non-operationalisable practice. As in Nakotte's idiosyncratic use of MT as artistic practice, the output of Pailthorpe's overstretching of Google translate transforms, in a way a 'consciousness-bound' translation loop could not, the translational procedure into a self-referential movement that marks a space of fundamental, non-rationalisable, black-boxed otherness within the textual fabric produced. This otherness still stands in relation to the foreign text opposite, but in a relationality freed from the burden of representation of that predecessor, existing as a presentation of itself solely: Translation as an art, not as a math problem.

References

Apter, E. (2006): The Translation Zone: A New Comparative Literature, Princeton: Princeton University Press.

Bajohr, H. (2022): "Artifizielle und postartifizielle Texte. Über Literatur und Künstliche Intelligenz". Retrieved from https://hannesbajohr.de/walter-hoellerer-vorlesung/.

Bender, E. et al. (2021): "On the Dangers of Stochastic Parrots. Can Language Models be too big?". Retrieved from https://dl.acm.org/doi/10.1145/3442188.3445922.

Brodersen, I. (2022): "Technik und Literaturübersetzen—willkommen im 21. Jahrhundert." Konterbande Magazin. Retrieved from https://babelwerk.de/essay/technik-und-literaturuebersetzen-willkommen-im-21-jahrhundert/.

Cayley, J. (2018): "Weapons of the Deconstructive Masses (WDM): Whatever Electronic Literature May or May Not Mean." In: Cayley, J.: Grammalepsy: Essays on Digital Language Art. New York: Bloomsbury Academic.

Celan, P. (1960): [Letter to Werner Weber]. Cited from Gellhaus, A. et al. (1997), 'Fremde Nähe'. Celan als Übersetzer, Marbach a. N.: Deutsche Schillergesellschaft.

Chamberlain, L. (1988): "Gender and Metaphorics of Translation." Signs 13/3, pp. 454–472.

Cramer, F. (2011): Exe.cut[up]able statements. Poetische Kalküle und Phantasmen des selbstausführenden Texts, Paderborn: Fink.

DuPoint, Q. (2018): "The Cryptological Origins of Machine Translation: From al-Kindi to Weaver". Amodern 8: Translation-Machination 01/2018, unpaginated. Retrieved from https://amodern.net/article/cryptological-origins-machine-translation/.

Dzieza, J. (2022): "The Great Fiction of AI." The Verge (20 July 2022). Retrieved from https://www.theverge.com/c/23194235/ai-fiction-writing-amazon-kindle-sudowrite-jasper.

Gramling, D. (2016): The Invention of Monolingualism, New York/ London: Bloomsbury Academic.

Höllerer, W. (1961): "Diese Zeitschrift hat ein Programm." Sprache im technischen Zeitalter 1 (1961), pp. 1–2.

Jakobson, R. (1959): "Linguistic Aspects of Translation." In: Brower, R. A. (Ed.), On Translation, Cambridge, MA: Harvard University Press, pp. 232–239.

Kenny, D. (2018): "Machine Translation." In: Rawling, P./ Wilson, P.: *Routledge Handbook on Translation and Philosophy*, Abingdon: Routledge, pp. 428–445.

Lewis-Kraus, G. (2015): "Is Translation an Art or a Math Problem." *The New York Times* (4 June 2015). Retrieved from https://www.nytimes.com/2015/06/07/magazine/is-translation-an-art-or-a-math-problem.html.

Locke, W.N./Booth, A.D. (1955): *Machine Translation of Languages*, Cambridge, MA/New York/London: The Technology Press of Massachusetts Institute of Technology, John Wiley & Sons and Chapman & Hall.

Luhn, A. (2022): Spiel mit Einsatz. Experimentelle Übersetzung als Praxis der Kritik, Wien/Berlin: Turia + Kant.

Mitchell, C. (2010): "Translating and Materiality: The Paradox of Visible Translation." Spectator 30/1, pp. 23–29, 25.

Mitchell, C. (2018): "Whether Something Works: Finding the Human in the Margins of Machine Translation." Amodern 8: Translation-Machination 01/2018, unpaginated. Retrieved from https://amodern.net/article/whether-something-works/.

Nakotte, J. (2021): "Sinn." Kurze 04, p. 33

Raley, R. (2003): "Machine Translation and Global English." The Yale Journal of Criticism 16/3, pp. 291–313.

Raley, R. (2016): "Algorithmic Translation." The New Centennial Review 16/1, pp. 115–137.

Slater, A. (2018): "Crypto-Monolingualism: Machine Translation and the Poetics of Automation," Amodern 8: Translation-Machination (01/2018), unpaginated. Retrieved from https://amodern.net/article/crypto-monolingualism/.

Strasser, M. (2020), Kannibalogie, Wien/Berlin: Turia + Kant.

Venuti, L. (1995/2008): The Translator's Invisibility. A History of Translation, London/New York: Routledge.

Weaver, W. (1949): Translation, New York: The Rockefeller Foundation.

Zemanek, H. (1961): "Möglichkeiten und Grenzen der automatischen Sprachübersetzung." Sprache im technischen Zeitalter 1, pp. 3–15.

Ревзин, И./Розенцвейг, В. (1964): Основы общего и машинного перевода, Moscow. [Isaac Revzin/Victor J. Rosenzweig: Fundamentals of General and Machine Translation]

Literature Survey

Literature Survey
1950s to the Present

Mathias Fuchs

This is an attempt to compare two waves of publications both dealing with the use of digital computers in the arts. The first bunch of publications was written in between 1956 and 1988. The second group consists of publications written in the current century and encompasses the years 2003 to 2021. The selection of texts is not complete and is biased by the author's collection of books in his bookshelves. One could claim that algorithmic art had two hype-cycles, that had different and particular ideas about what the problems with using computers in the arts were, in what way the algorithms performed various tasks, what the role of the artist was and what the impact on society and everyday life was. It is also interesting to observe what key notions have been used in describing related questions.

In the 1960s and 1970s frequent notions in book titles have been "computer", "information", "telecommunication", "kinetic" and "cybernetics". These notions became rare at the turn of the century and have been replaced with key notions of "algorithm", "data", "machine learning" and "AI". It is possible that a post-digital society tends to not mention the computer, as almost everything is computerised. It is also possible that cybernetics and communication theory had their golden days when "Control and Communication" (Wiener 1948) posed a threat and a promise to modern societies. The military interest in cybernetics met eyeball to eyeball with politically motivated expectations of a "cybernetic revolution" and guerrilla media (Gene Youngblood, Michael Shamberg amongst others, cf. the article by Angela Krewani in this journal). Today's ubiquitous phrase of algorithmic art and generative art was in the 1960s usually referred to as "computer art" (—with Frieder Nake being the exception).

It is actually quite surprising that the term computer instead of algorithmic was predominantly used in regard to digital art. This terminological choice suggests a predominance of the technical device over the process. The majority of 1960s and 1970s artists stated that the programme (or what we now call the algorithm) was more relevant to the works created than the hardware: the computer. To paraphrase Hans Ulrich Reck's mockery that we should not speak about "oil art" when we talk about landscape paintings (Reck 2007: 17), we could also say that we should not speak about "computer art" when we talk about work that is algorithmically produced. When looking at the code that computer artists of the 1960s wrote, this code is obviously of an algorithmic nature in the sense computer scientists understand algorithms. Today however, the procedures and processes used by artists are rather applications of complex underlying software structures. The user has no chance to understand what exactly the clusters of routines and subroutines do. Not even programmers who have been employed to write parts of the tens of thousands of lines can say, how the systems behave in the end and have to rely on assumptions of what the software might produce as a result. The so-called algorithms of contemporary algorithmic art are therefore not algorithms in the strict sense of a transparent linear sequence of operations written to accomplish verifiable and repeatable results. They are rather big data analyses that take for granted what a majority of data donors leave as a digital footprint when searching for information, building webpages or replying to customer satisfaction polls (cf. Rethinking AI: Neural Networks, Biometrics and the New Artificial Intelligence, by Reichert and Fuchs in the Journal of Digital Culture and Society 2018)

Frieder Nake, in his early texts from the 1960s, is an exception for the terminology used in the 1960s, when he states that artistic practice consists of working on the algorithms as the essential material of art. He goes so far as to call the modern artists "algorists" (cf. the article by Christa Sommerer and Laurent Mignonneau in this issue of the journal).

Fig. 1: Publications by Horst Völz (1988), Herbert W. Franke (1978) and Abraham A. Moles (1973): Computer and Art, Art versus Technology? or Art and Computer.

With book covers featuring fractal geometry, pixilation and random pattern generators the discourse on computers and the arts was fuelled by a confrontation and a possible harmonisation of science, technology and avant-garde art. C.P. Snow's *Two Cultures* (1959) affected the awareness of the problem. The titles by the above books published in the German Democratic Republic and in the Federal Republic of Germany theorize computational methods as tools for the artist or even as systems replacing the individual artists. Some of the authors of the 1960s favoured the idea that the computer could be a "complexity amplifier" (German: Komplexitätsverstärker) and the artworks produced should be called "computer-aided art" whereas others praised the machine as true creator and a device for a democratisation of the arts that would allow every art lover to get his or her personal art piece. Not only would this destroy the myth of the one and only masterpiece that could be sold at a horrendous price, but it would also by the means of artistic mass production empower the masses to have a share of the formerly exclusive art world.

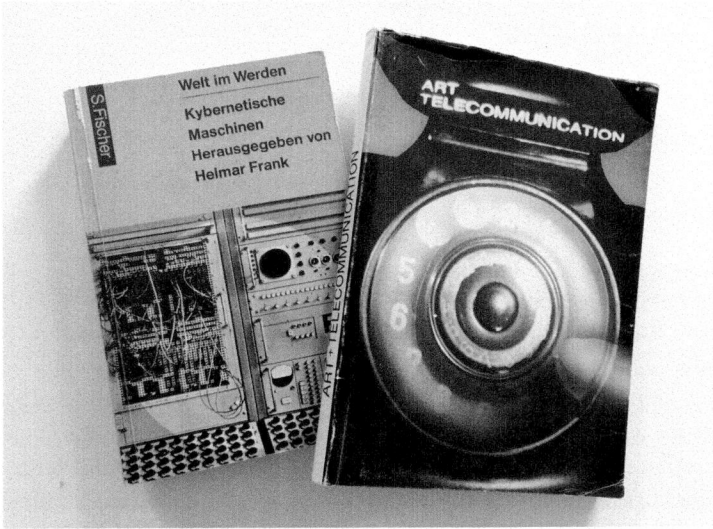

Fig. 2: Publications by Helmar Frank (1964) and Heidi Grundmann (1984)

Margit Rosen (2011) speaks about the computer as a "thinking machine" that has been adopted as an artistic tool. Art, according to her observations, becomes "visual research". The title of her book, *A Little-Known Story About a Movement […]*, refers to very early computer graphic experiments in Yugoslavia. The series of international exhibitions in Zagreb called *Nove tendencije* started in 1961 and is just one, yet an important piece of evidence, that early computer art did not exclusively stem from the big industrial research centres of Bell Labs, SIEMENS or IBM, but that an avant-garde movement using computing machinery had its roots in countries like the Soviet Union (Konstantinow 2018), Yugoslavia, Chile and Brazil as much as in the USA, France and West Germany (cf. Konstantinow about computer animation and Soviet kinetic art of the 1960s and the article by Giselle Beiguelman in this issue of the journal).

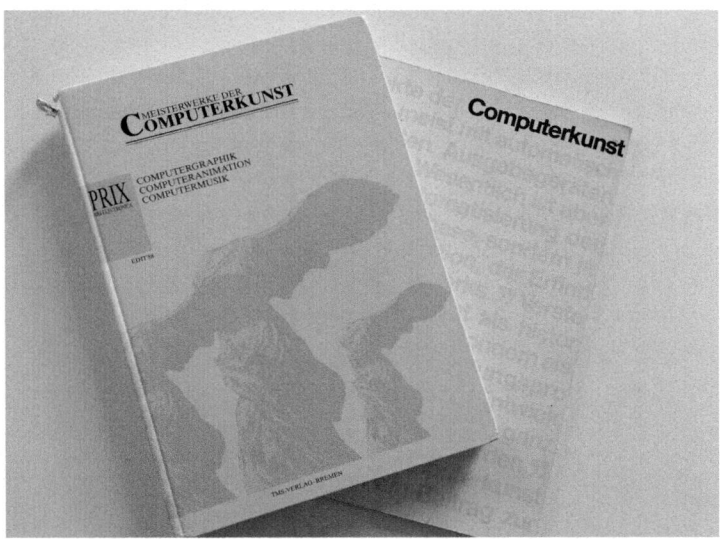

Fig. 3: Publications by Hannes Leopoldseder (ed.) (1988) and IBM Germany (1975)

The Linz based *ars electronica* festival has been an important showcase for algorithmic art since 1979. The early publications declare the artistic sub-disciplines of computer art as computer graphics, computer animation and computer music. This was before Game Art, AI text generation, Virtual Reality, algorithmic processes for performance pieces, or 3D computer prints entered the stage.

There have been graphics of a representative character, but a large section of computer art of the 1960s and 70s was abstract (Vera Molnar, Manfred Mohr, Herbert W. Franke, Groupe Art et Informatique de Vincennes, Patrick Greussay a.o.).

Greussay finds an interesting point of view, when asked whether it is him or the algorithm that creates the artwork. He states: "I am neither master nor slave of my programme." (Greussay in: IBM 1975: 47) On the one hand the programme defines a visual line sequence that is determined by an algorithm. On the other hand Patrick Greussay keeps the decision to himself of when to stop the computer drawing. Different to that Pierre-Louis Neumann watches a graphic AI programme rendering endless numbers of visualisations (ibid.: 49). But he does not want to delegate the process of plotting out the results to a machine. He does this by hand. "Of cause it would be possible to have the computer visualize the ideas that I coded in the programme. But that would mean that I transferred the job of 'painting an artwork' to the computer. But being a painter myself, I insist on keeping the complete freedom of interpreting what the computer suggests. That's why I paint with my own hands. The programme may motivate me, but it is not my director." (ibid.) Similar strategies to the one Pierre-Louis Neumann adopts, can be found in the realm of computer music production.

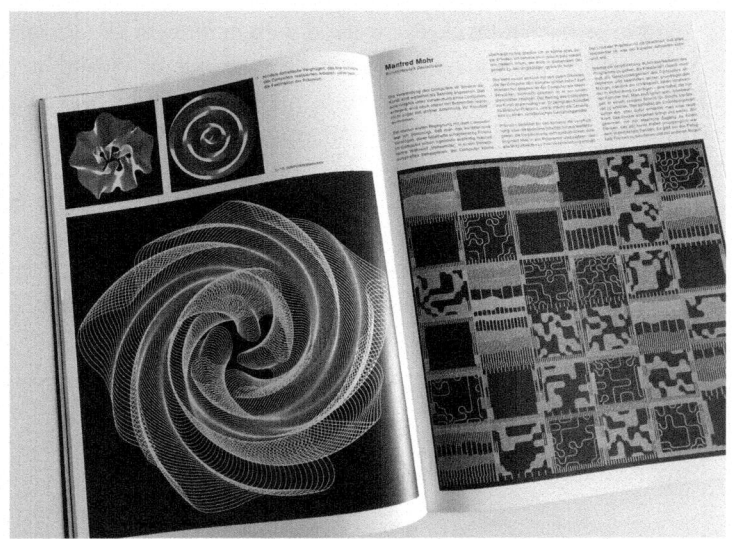

Fig. 4: Pages 38 and 39 from Computerkunst by IBM Germany (1975)

Fig. 5: Publications by Heinz von Foerster (1969), John Snell (1978) and Lejaren A. Hiller (1963)

Lejaren Hiller was one of the composers who used mainframe computers to generate scores for musical instruments. His composition method was based on parameters from classical communication theory like information content, redundancy and probability distribution. The *ILLIAC Suite for string quartet* (Hiller and Isaacson 1956), named after the computer at the University of Illinois, and his *Electronic Study No.4* (Hiller and Baker 1961 - 62) are based on generative algorithms.

Hiller is proud to state that he closely worked with engineers like Robert Baker, a research assistant at the university whom he mentions as co-author. Hiller's composition was generated on an IBM 7094 mainframe, but it was played and interpreted by human musicians. The programme MUSICOMP (MUsic-Simulator-Interpreter for COMpositional Procedures) generated the text output that was then translated into musical notation. It is obvious that traditional musicians who had to play the piece, interpreted performance instructions like *allegro con brio*, *adagio*, *crescendo* and *diminuendo* in a way they had been trained by instrumental music practice. The auditory experience of the performance can therefore be said to have been characterised by input from both man and machine.

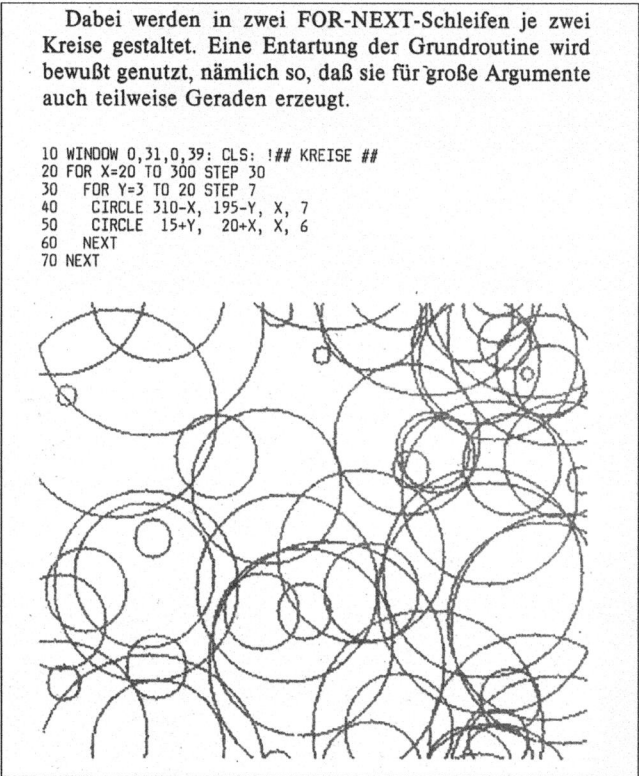

Fig. 6: *Code example for computer art by Horst Völz (1988)*

In his later compositions Hiller tried to eliminate interpretative nuance and delegated the sound production to computer hardware as well. Even so Hiller's pieces of computer music still rely on the composer/programmer as the master of the compositional process. The machine just follows the algorithms provided by the human: on the level of structural organisation and on the level of sound production. Recent approaches give away far more decision-making power to Artificial Intelligence and Big Data analyses. One route that computer music takes at present is an interesting branch of AI techniques called genetic programming, a recent technique in the field of computer science for "automatic programming" of computers (Alpern 1995). Rather than basing its grammar on score input to the computer, genetic programming generates its own musical materials as well as it forms its own grammar. It is obvious that the days when algorithmic art could be produced by a few lines of code have gone. (See code example in Fig. 6)

I think it is fair to say that comparably simple and transparent algorithms of the 1960s and 1970s triggered complex and diverse discourse about algorithmic culture, the role of the "algorists" and the impact of computer art on society and everyday life. Today we are faced with complexity at an extremely high level to technically generate computer art. Let's hope that the discourse on algorithmic art matches the sophistication of the code.

References (a) 1956 to 1988

Ascott, Roy (1983): La plissure du texte. In: Electra exhibition catalogue, Paris.
Bense, Max (1956): Aesthetische Information. aesthetica II. Krefeld, Baden-Baden: Agis-Verlag.
Bense, Max (1998): "Einführung in die informationsästhetische Ästhetik." In: Max Bense (ed.) Ausgewählte Schriften: Bd. 3: Ästhetik und Texttheorie. Stuttgart: Agis-Verlag, pp. 251–417.
Frank, Helmar (1964): Kybernetische Maschinen. Prinzip und Anwendung der automatischen Nachrichtenverarbeitung. S. Fischer Verlag, Frankfurt am Main.
Franke, H. W. (1985): The New Visual Age: The Influence of Computer Graphics on Art and Society, in: *Leonardo*, The MIT Press Vol. 18, No. 2,
Franke, Herbert W. (1978): Kunst kontra Technik? Wechselwirkungen zwischen Kunst, Naturwissenschaft und Technik. Fischer, Frankfurt am Main.
Franke, Herbert W. (1984): Computer Grafik. Galerie. Bilder nach Programm. Kunst im elektronischen Zeitalter. Köln: Du Mont Schauberg.
Grundmann, Heidi (ed.) (1984): Art and Telecommunication. Western Front Publications, Vancouver.
Hiller, Lejaren A. (1963): Informationstheorie und Computermusik. In: Darmstädter Beiträge zur Neuen Musik. B. Schott's Söhne, Mainz.
IBM Deutschland (ed.) (1975): Computerkunst. IBM Deutschland GmbH, Stuttgart.
Leopoldseder, Hannes (ed.) (1988): Meisterwerke der Computerkunst. TMS Verlag, Bremen.
Moles, Abraham A. (1973): Kunst & Computer. DuMont Schauberg, Köln.
Popper, Frank (1968): Origins and Development of Kinetic Art. New York Graphic Society, Ltd, Greenwich, Connecticut.

Snell, John (ed.) (1978): Computer Music Journal. Vol. II, No. 1, People's Computer Company, Menlo Park.

Völz, Horst (1988): Computer und Kunst. Urania Verlag, Leipzig, Jena and Berlin.

von Foerster, Heinz/Beauchamp, James W. (eds.) (1969): Music by Computers. John Wiley and Sons, New York, London, Sydney and Toronto.

Wiener, Norbert (1964): Cybernetics or Control and Communication in the Animal and the Machine. MIT Press 1948.

References (b) 2003 to 2021

Alpern, Adam (1995): Techniques for algorithmic composition of music. Hampshire College. http://alum.hampshire.edu/~adaF92/algocomp/algocomp95.html

Ascott, Roy (2003): "Behaviourist Art and the Cybernetic Vision." Edward R. Shanken (ed.): Roy Ascott. Telematic Embrace. Visionary Theories of Art, Technology and Consciousness, Berkeley, Los Angeles: University of California Press, pp. 109-56.

Audry, Sofian (2021): Art in the Age of Machine Learning, Cambridge: MIT Press.

Block, Friedrich W./ Heibach, Christiane/Wenz, Karin (eds.) (2004): *poesis. Ästhetik digitaler Poesie*. Ostfildern: Hatje Cantz 2004.

Bown, Oliver (2018): "Performer interaction and expectation with live algorithms: experiences with 'Zamyatin'." In: Digital Creativity, 29(1), pp. 37-50.

Bucher, Taina (2018): If...Then: Algorithmic power and politics. Oxford University

Caramiaux, B./Donnarumma, M. (2021): "Artificial Intelligence in Music and Performance: A Subjective Art-Research Inquiry". In: E. R. Miranda (ed.), Handbook of Artificial Intelligence for Music. Foundations, Advanced Approaches, and Developments for Creativity. London: Springer, pp. 75-95.

Christie's (2018): "Is artificial intelligence set to become art's next medium?" https://www.christies.com/features/a-collaboration-between-two-artists-one-human-one-a-machine-9332-1.aspx

Cox, D. (2006): Metaphoric Mappings: The Art of Visualization, in: *Aesthetic Computing*, Cambridge, MA: MIT Press.

Dourish, Paul (2016): "Algorithms and their others: Algorithmic culture in context." Big Data & Society 3/2. https://doi.org/10.1177/2053951716665128

Eckermann, Sylvia (ed.) (2014): Algorithmisiert. Czernin Verlag, Wien.

Fishwick, P. (2006): *Aesthetic Computing*, Cambridge, MA: MIT Press.

Fuchs, Mathias/Reichert, Rámon (2018): Rethinking AI: Neural Networks, Biometrics and the New Artificial Intelligence. Digital Culture & Society (DCS): Vol. 4, Issue 1, transcript Verlag, Bielefeld.

Galloway, Alexander R. (2006): Gaming: Essays on algorithmic culture, Minnesota: Minnesota University Press.

Konstantinow, Nikolai (2019): Ankunft einer Katze. Geschichte und Theorie der ersten Computersimulation eines Lebewesens. ciconia ciconia, Berlin.

Mersch, Dieter (2019): "Kreativität und Künstliche Intelligenz. Einige Bemerkungen zu einer Kritik algorithmischer Rationalität." In: ZfM Zeitschrift für Medienwissenschaft 11/2, pp. 65–74. https://doi.org/10.25969/MEDIAREP/12634

Nake, F. (2012): Construction and Intuition: Creativity in Early Computer Art, in: *Computers and Creativity*, McCormack, J. and d´Inverno, M. (Eds.) Springer Verlag, Berlin Heidelberg

Piehler, Heike (2002): Die Anfänge der Computerkunst. Frankfurt/Main: dot-Verl. Dr. Dotzler Medien-Institut.

Reck, Hans Ulrich (2007): The Myth of Media Art. The Aesthetics of the Techno/Imaginary and an Art Theory of Virtual Realities. Verlag für Geisteswissenschaften, Weimar.

Rosen, Margit in cooperation with Peter Weibel, Darko Fritz and Marija Gattin (ed.) (2011): A Little-Known Story About a Movement, a Magazine, and the Computer's Arrival in Art. New Tendencies and Bit International, 1961–1973. MIT Press, Cambridge, Massachusetts.

Scorzin, Pamela (2021): "Kann KI Kunst sein? AI ART: Neue Positionen, technisierte Ästhetiken von Mensch und Maschine". In: Kunstforum International 278/4, p 48.

Snow, Charles Percy (2001) [1959]: The Two Cultures. London: Cambridge University Press.

Striphas, Ted (2015): "Algorithmic culture." European Journal of Cultural Studies, 18/4-5, pp. 395-412.

Zylinska, J. (2020): AI Art. Machine Visions and Warped Dreams. London: Open Humanities Press.

Biographical Notes

Giselle Beiguelman is an artist and Professor at the Faculty of Architecture, Urbanism, and Design at the University of São Paulo.

Simon Biggs is Professor of Art and Director of the South Australian School of Art at the University of South Australia. He is a new media artist working with interactive and generative systems, and writes on the theory, practice and history of new media.

Patricia de Vries is a research professor at the Gerrit Rietveld Academie. Her research focuses on artistic practices that intervene in capitalist enclosures.

Marco Donnarumma is a media and performance artist, director, composer and scholar.

Mathias Fuchs is an artist, musician and media scholar. He is the director of the Gamification Lab at Leuphana University in Lüneburg. He is a pioneer in the field of game art and is a leading scholar in game studies.

Sue Hawksley received her PhD in dance, technology and philosophy from the University of Edinburgh. She is a dance artist and Director of interdisciplinary performance company Articulate Animal.

Angela Krewani is Professor of Media Studies at the University of Marburg. Her research focuses on media art, digital cultures and imaging in the natural sciences, including biomedicine and nanotechnology.

Anna Luhn is a postdoctoral researcher at the Cluster of Excellence Temporal Communities: Doing Literature in a Global Perspective, Freie Universität Berlin.

Mark McDonnell is Adjunct Associate Professor at the University of South Australia, a Machine Learning Specialist and Chief Technology Officer.

Christa Sommerer and **Laurent Mignonneau** are internationally renowned media artists, researchers and pioneers of interactive art. Sommerer studied botany and anthropology at the University of Vienna and sculpture at the University of Fine Arts Vienna. Laurent Mignonneau studied video art at the Academy of Fine Arts

Angouleme, France. They run the master and doctoral study course "Interface Cultures" at the University of Art and Industrial Design in Linz.

Karin Wenz is an assistant professor of Digital Cultures at Maastricht University, Netherlands.

[transcript]

WISSEN. GEMEINSAM. PUBLIZIEREN.

transcript pflegt ein mehrsprachiges transdisziplinäres Programm mit Schwerpunkt in den Kultur- und Sozialwissenschaften. Aktuelle Beiträge zu Forschungsdebatten werden durch einen Fokus auf Gegenwartsdiagnosen und Zukunftsthemen sowie durch innovative Bildungsmedien ergänzt. Wir ermöglichen eine Veröffentlichung in diesem Programm in modernen digitalen und offenen Publikationsformaten, die passgenau auf die individuellen Bedürfnisse unserer Publikationspartner*innen zugeschnitten werden können.

UNSERE LEISTUNGEN IN KÜRZE

- partnerschaftliche Publikationsmodelle
- Open Access-Publishing
- innovative digitale Formate: HTML, Living Handbooks etc.
- nachhaltiges digitales Publizieren durch XML
- digitale Bildungsmedien
- vielfältige Verknüpfung von Publikationen mit Social Media

Besuchen Sie uns im Internet: www.transcript-verlag.de

Unsere aktuelle Vorschau finden Sie unter: www.transcript-verlag.de/vorschau-download